フランク・ロイド・ライト

旧山邑邸
ヨドコウ迎賓館

1924 芦屋

Frank Lloyd Wright
Yamamura House
Yodoko Guest House

Text:Masami Tanigawa   Photos:Kazuyoshi Miyamoto

Banana Books

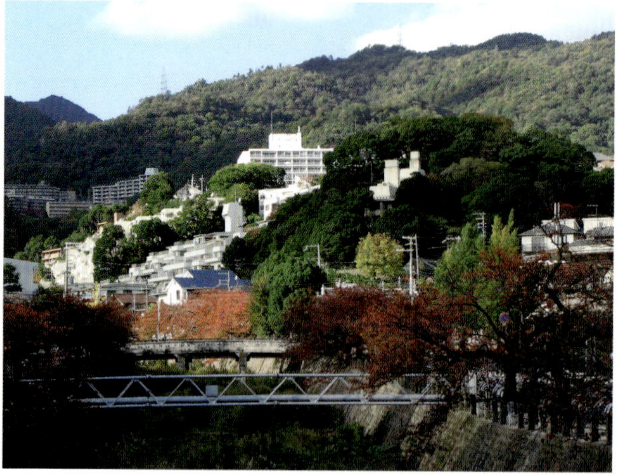

旧山邑邸・ヨドコウ迎賓館

Yamamura House
Yodoko Guest House

目 次

◇住宅写真	4-35
◇図面	30-31, 42-45
◇ディティール	38-41
◇生き続ける大谷石住宅の奇跡	
電車のホームから望める洋館	46
少壮住宅作家、ライト	48
文化財指定へ	50
旧山邑邸の特徴	50
ライトが受けた日本建築の影響	56
重要文化財、旧山邑邸	56
保存意識の困難を克服して	60

Contents

◇Photos of the Yamamura House	4-35
◇Drawings	30-31, 42-45
◇Details	38-41
◇The miracle of the surviving Oya Stone House	
Western-style building visible from the Train Platform	47
Wright in his prime as a residential architect	49
Designation as a Cultural Property	51
Features of the Yamamura House	51
The influence of Japanese Architecture on Wright	57
Important Cultural Property, the Yamamura House	57
Overcoming the Difficulties of Conservation Consciousness	61

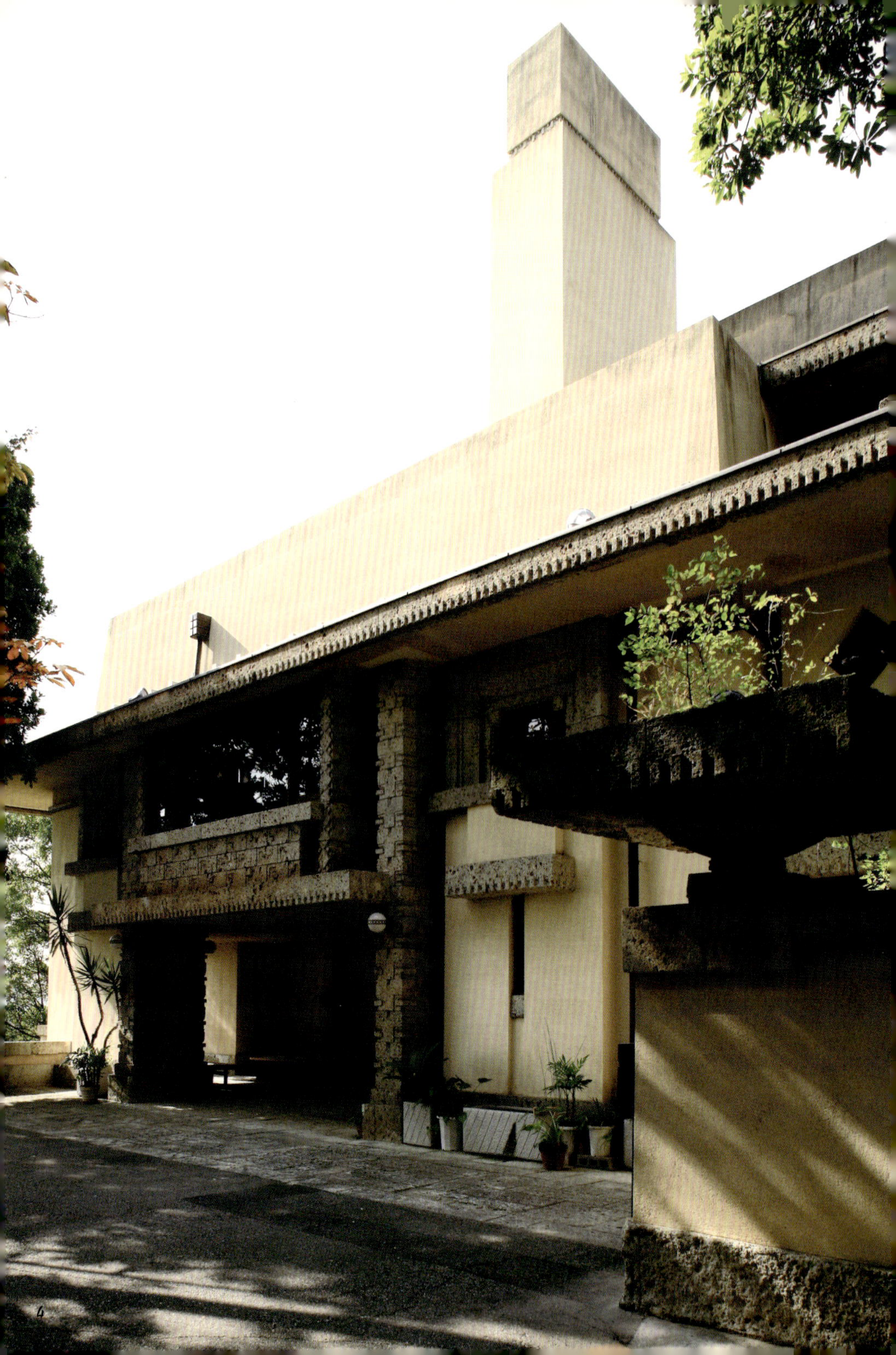

▶ 玄関は、左右対称。幾何学模様の刻みがある大谷石の豊かな装飾に迎えられる。上部には2階応接室の嵌め殺しの大窓。
The entrance is symmetric.
A rich decoration of Oya stone with geometric engravings welcomes you. A large non-opening window in the 2nd floor salon is above.

▶ 玄関手前の花台も大谷石造り。アメリカでは垂れ下がる植物を置くことが多い。
The flower pot before the entrance is also made of Oya stone. In the US, it is usual to use hanging plants.

◀ 長いアプローチの末、最南端、大谷石を敷き詰めた床の車寄せ（玄関）に到着。
A long approach finally takes you to the car entrance at the south end covered with Oya stone.

5

▲ 玄関部分、中央部に水が流れる仕掛けがある。左側の奥まったところが玄関。扉は狭く密やかに造られ、大人一人が通るほどの幅しかない。左：玄関詳細。

There is a courseway for water flow in the center of the entrance. The entrance is in the back of the left side. The door is narrow and hidden. Left: entrance detail.

▶ 玄関に入ると直ぐに上階へと導く階段がある。建設当時より靴履きの生活をしていたのか、玄関の床部分から階段まで段差のないまま大谷石で造られている。

There is a stairway to the upper floors immediately at the entrance. The area from the entrance floor to the stairway is made of Oya stone and there is no step from the entrance to the first floor perhaps because shoes were worn inside the building since the time it was constructed.

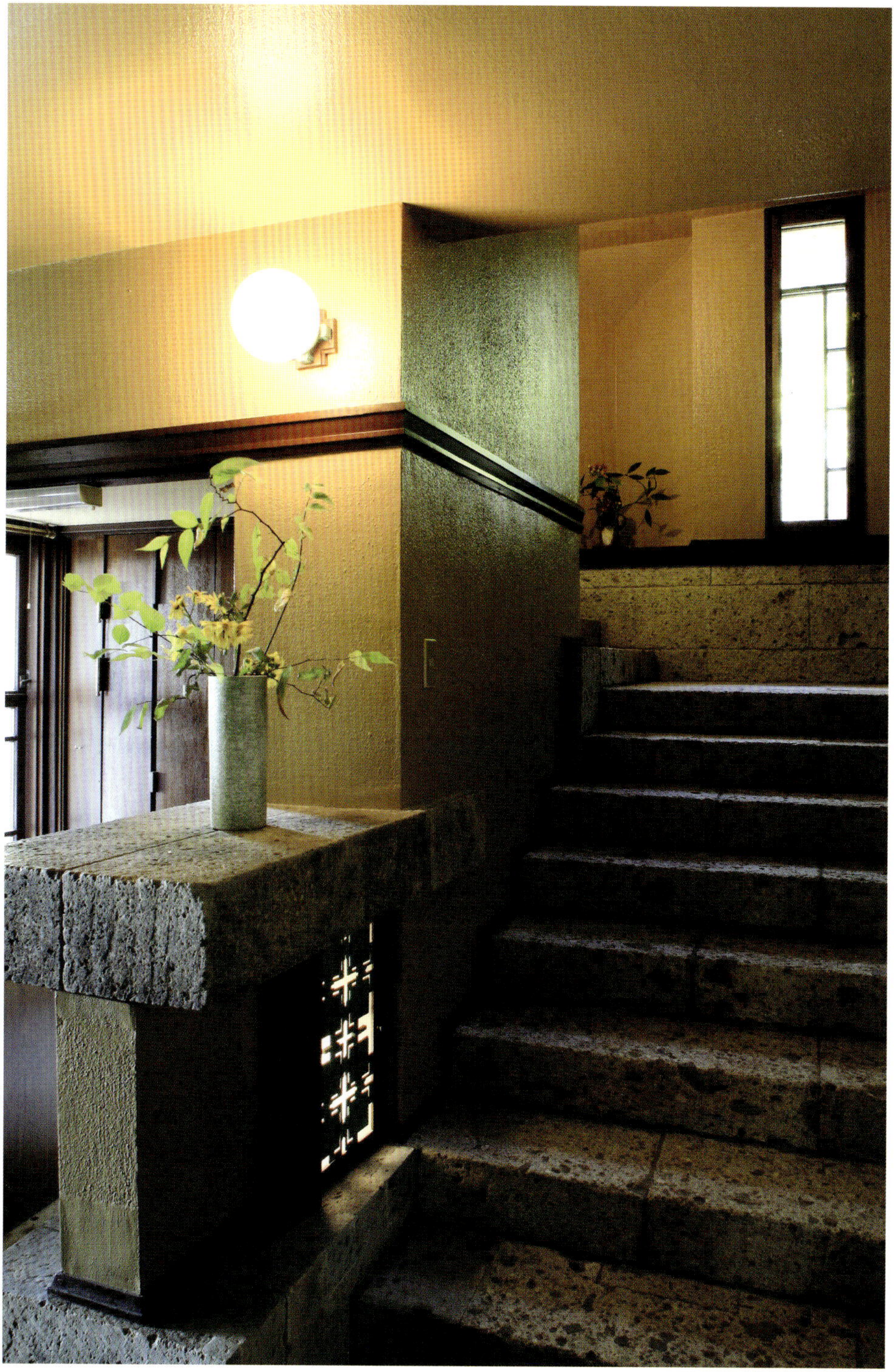

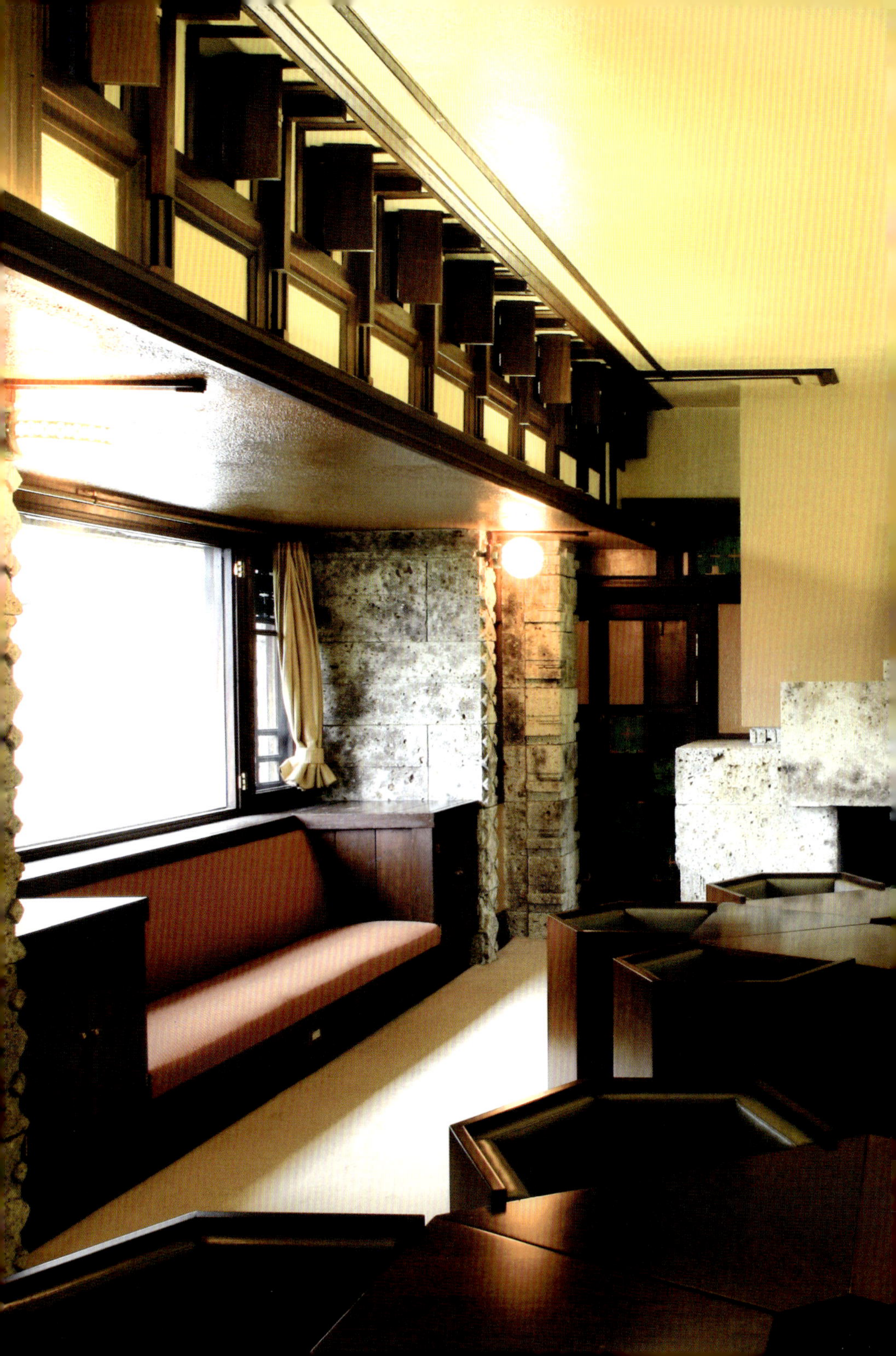

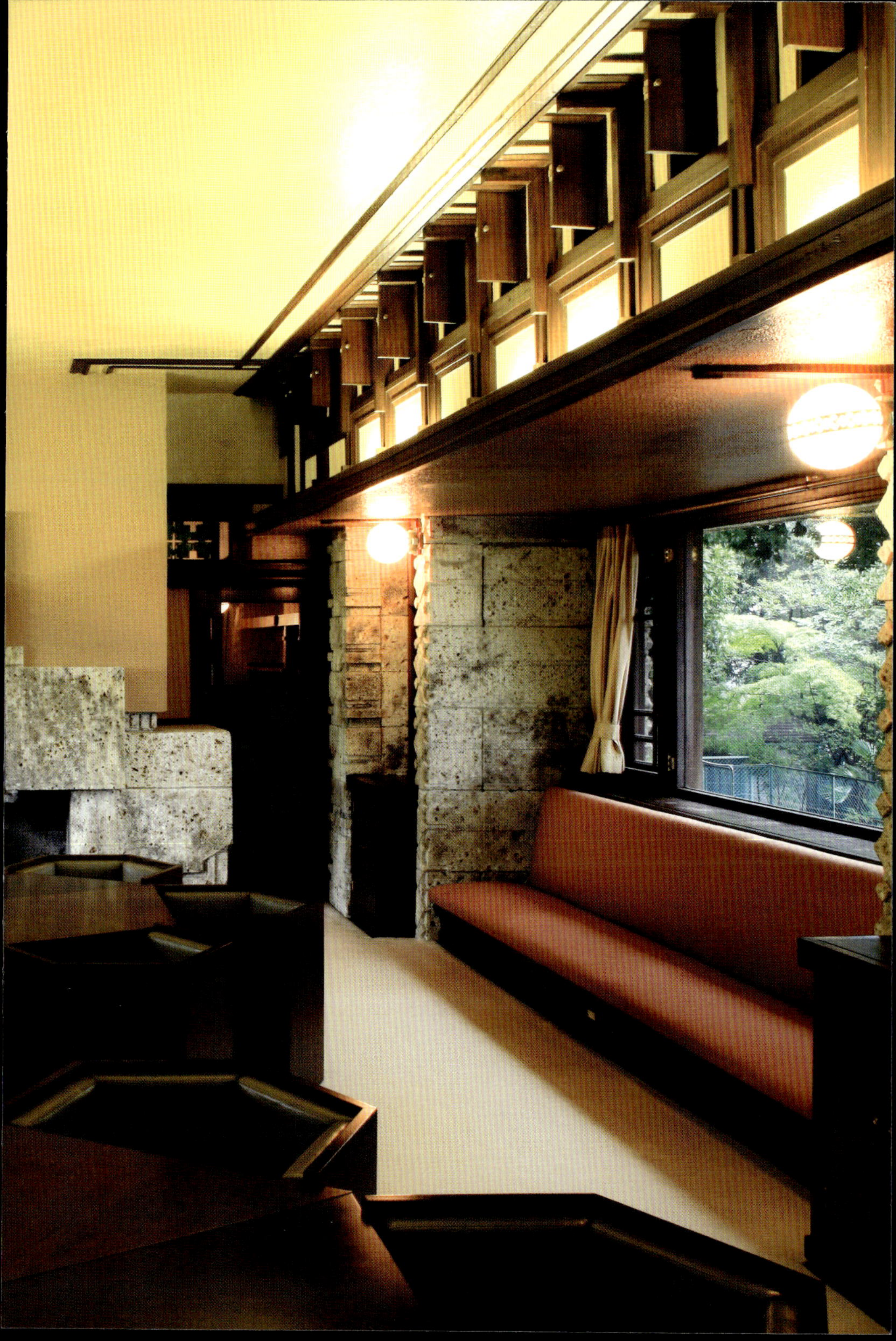

▲ 2階応接室北面、左右対称の端正なデザインで統一されている。二組ある机と椅子はオリジナルではない。上部に連続して設けられた高窓を開けると爽風が吹き抜けた。

The north side of the 2nd floor salon is integrated with a neat symmetrical design. The pairs of desks and chairs are not Wright's originals. A breeze blows in when a series of upper windows are opened.

▲ 応接室からバルコニーへの出入り口。
Doorway from the salon to the balcony.

▲ 応接室南のバルコニーのルーバーも大谷石造り。地震の際、柱がずれるなどの被害を受けたが現在は綺麗に補修されている。
The louver of the southern balcony of the 2nd floor salon is also made of Oya stone. Although there was earthquake damage such as displacement of columns, they are now repaired.

10

2階応接室を南向きに見る。高低二重の天井は、折り上げ天井の影響を受けている。低い天井に間接照明が設置され、高い天井を照らす。現在は、高窓にガラスが嵌められて開かない。

Looking southward at the 2nd floor salon. The tray ceiling is probably influenced by the Japanese "oriage" ceiling style. The ambient lights are set in the lower ceiling to light the higher ceiling. The top windows are glazed and do not open.

▲ 応接室東面。玄関前の木々が室内の風景に取り込まれ、季節を感じさせてくれる。
East side of the 2nd floor salon. The surrounding trees incorporated into the interior scene, allow one to feel the seasons.

▲ 応接室から水屋に入る手前にある扉。狭いが外にでることが出来る。
Door between the salon and the service room. You can go outside through the door although it is narrow.

▲ 応接室の暖炉。大きい大谷石のシンプルなデザイン。
Fireplace of the 2nd floor salon. Simple design of large masonry of Oya stone.

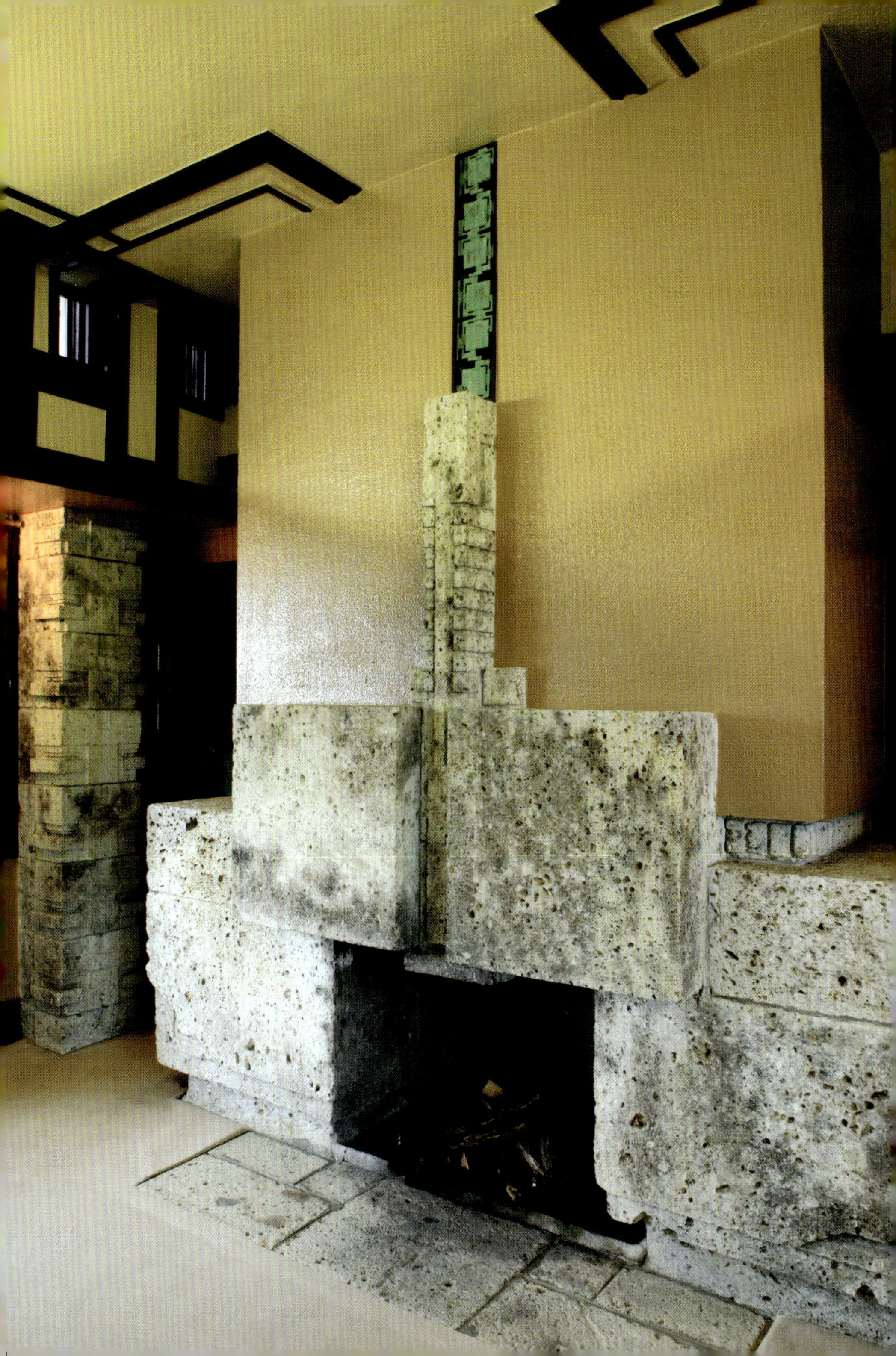

▶ 左手は1階から2階への踊り場。アルコーブに花が置かれて、床の間を思わせる造り。右手は、3階への階段。

The left side is a resting-place between the 1st and 2nd floors. A flower is put at the alcove, which is suggestive of the tokonoma, an alcove in a traditional Japanese room. The right side is the stairway to the 3rd floor.

▶ 3階西側の長い廊下より2階への踊り場を見る。ここで導線が二手に分かれ、奥の階段は、和室前室へ続く。

Looking from the long hallway on the 3rd floor at the resting-place between the 2nd and 3rd floors. The circulation is divided into two and the stairway behind continues to the front chamber of a Japanese-style rooms.

▲ 3階西側の廊下。窓に嵌め込まれた銅板の飾り金物のシルエットが美しく風景に重なる。
3rd floor hallway of the west side. The silhouette of decorative copper plates beautifully synchronizes with natural scenery.

▲ 連続する開口部から四季の景観が堪能でき、飾り金物のシルエットが床に影を落とす。
The silhouette of decorative copper plates beautifully synchronizes with natural scenery.

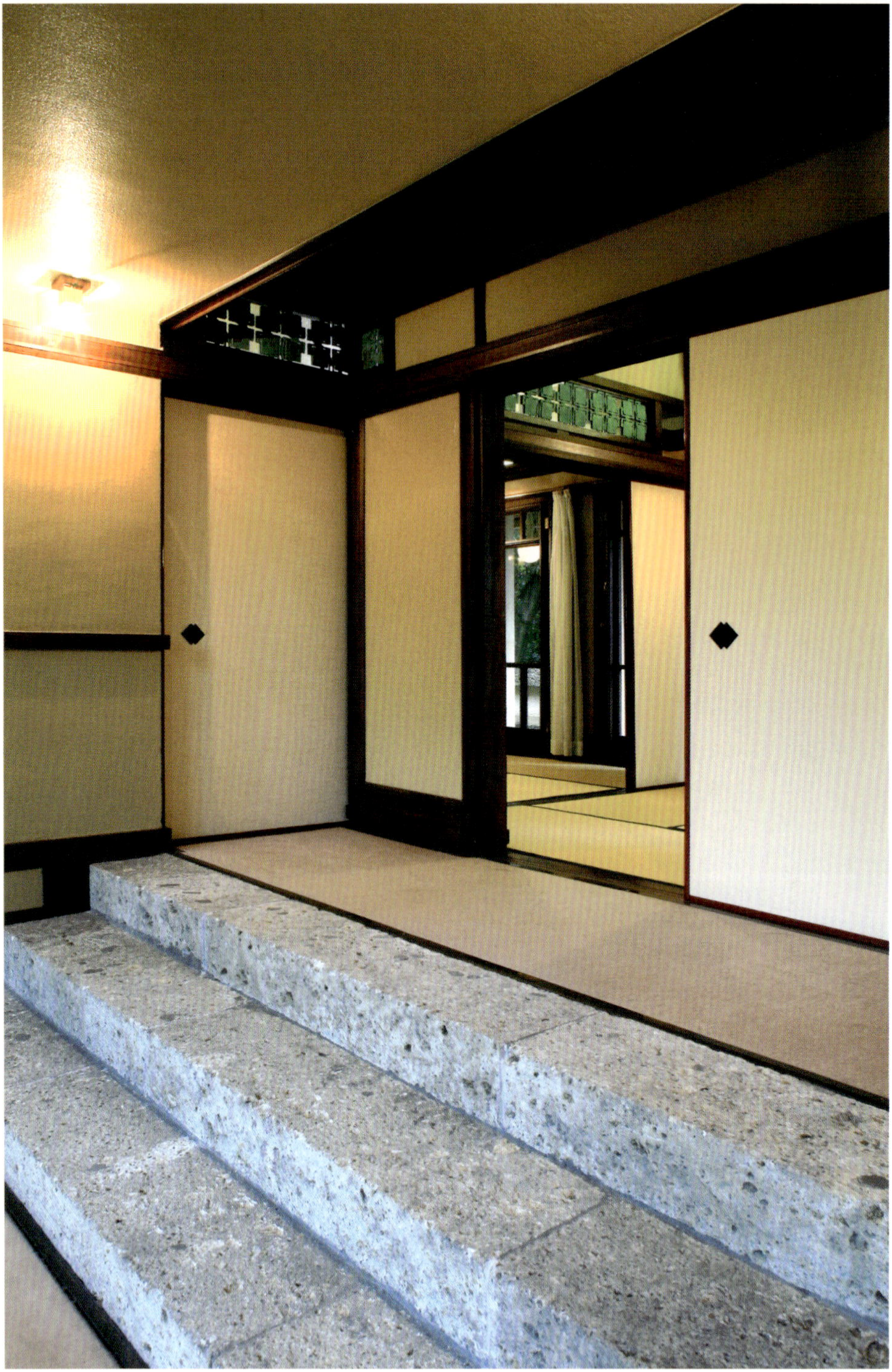

▲ 3階和室前室より北に和室が三間設けられている。手前より、八畳、六畳、十畳の構成。欄間に付けられた飾り金物が目をひく。右手は、バルコニーになっている。
There are three Japanese-style rooms north from the front chamber. From the foreground there are eight-mat, six-mat and ten-mat rooms. The transoms with decorative copper plates are very impressive. The right side is the balcony.

◀ 大谷石の階段から畳の敷かれた3階和室への入口は、ユニークな構成。
The approach has a unique composition from the Oya stone steps to the 3rd floor Japanese-style room.

▶ 3階和室（十畳）の床の間。和室（八畳）とは異なる構成。

3rd floor Japanese-style room (ten-mat), Tokonoma. Different composition from the eight-mat Japanese room.

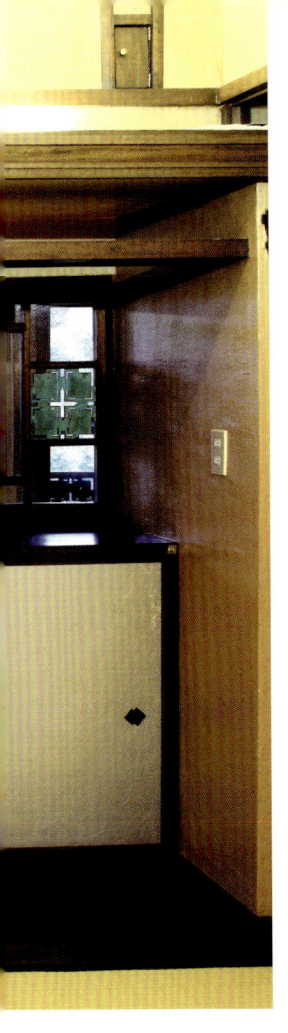

◀ 3階和室（八畳）、床の間と書院造り。上部には、応接室同様の高窓。現在は採光のみ可能。
3rd floor Japanese-style room (eight-mat). Tokonoma alcove in a traditional Japanese room and Shoin-zukuri, traditional style of Japanese residential architecture. There are high windows as in the salon. At present only natural lighting is possible.

▲ 木組みのしつらえに嵌め込まれた飾り金物が印象的。
Striking are the decorative copper plates on the timberwork fixtures.

▲ 3階和室前室の家族室。天井は低く抑えられているが、心地よい空間。3階屋上に続くガラス扉があるため明るい。
Front chamber of a Japanese-style room/family room on the 3rd floor. Comfortable space although the ceiling is lower. The room is bright due to the glazed door that leads to the rooftop.

▶ 3階和室奥の4階食堂につながる階段。各所に設けられた低い台座に植物が置かれると、室内に生気を与える。
Stairway behind the Japanese-style room on the 3rd floor. This stairway leads to the dining room on the 4th floor. The indoor space becomes full of vitality with plants on the low pedestals placed everywhere.

禁煙

▶ 3階洗面室。建設当時、設備は最先端のもので現在当たり前のようにみられる、温水と冷水の蛇口が、二組もついている。流しには、ガラス棒が水切り用に張られている。

Washing room on the 3rd floor. The equipment was leading-edge at that time and there are two pairs of water outlets for hot/cold water, which are usual these days. A glass rod is set in the sink for drying.

▶ 3階浴室、薄い朱色のタイル貼りの浴槽。

Bathroom on the 3rd floor. Bathtub with light vermilion tile.

▲ 3階浴室の換気、採光用窓が浴槽上部に設置されている。
Bathroom on the 3rd floor. Windows for natural lighting are set over the bathtub.

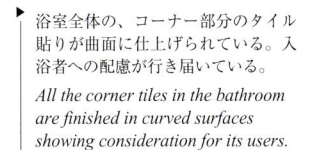

▶ 浴室全体の、コーナー部分のタイル貼りが曲面に仕上げられている。入浴者への配慮が行き届いている。
All the corner tiles in the bathroom are finished in curved surfaces showing consideration for its users.

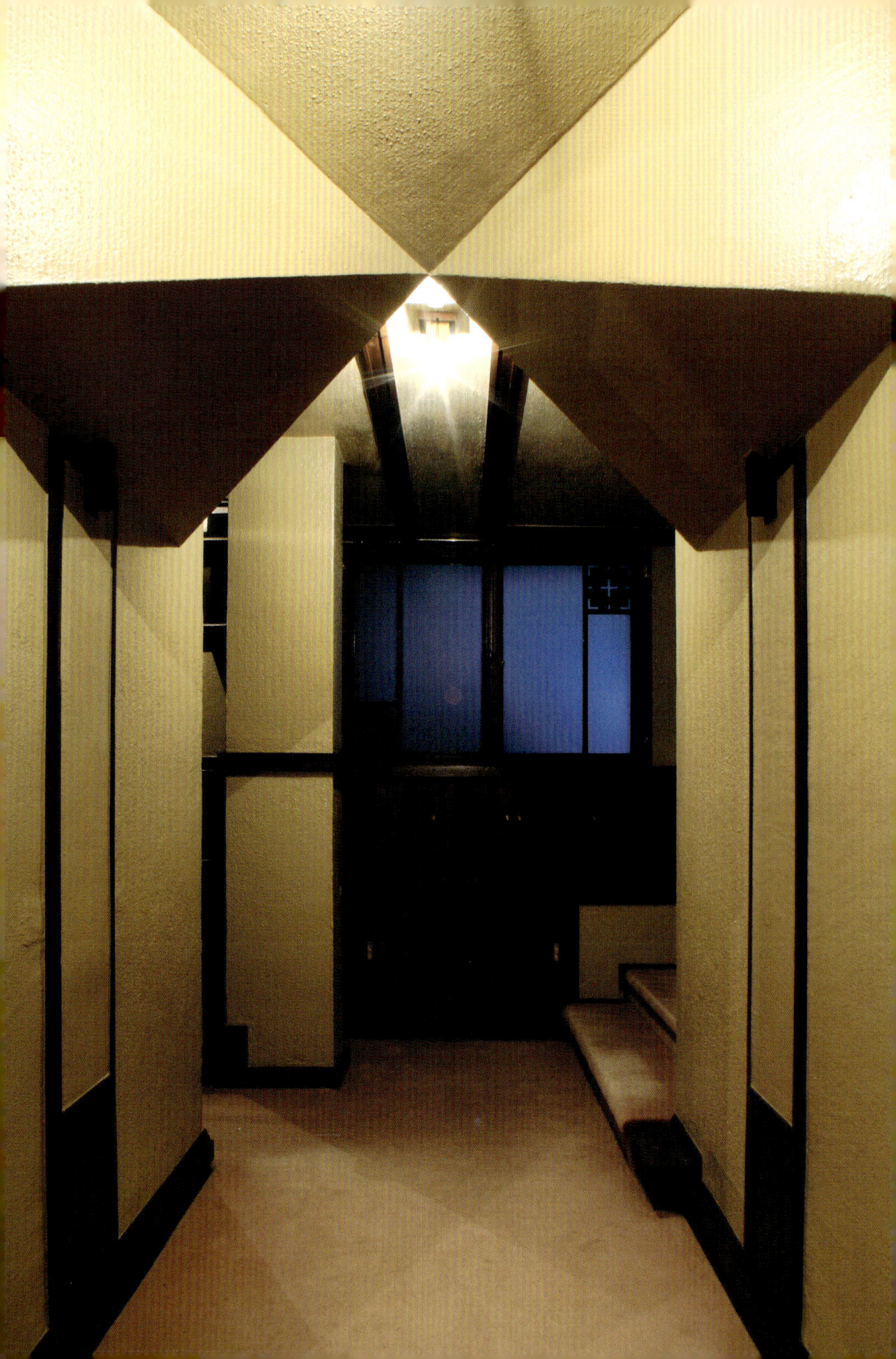

▸ 3階廊下より婦人室へは階段をあがる。右手は寝室とつながっており、座礼の空間と立礼の空間をつなぐための構成になっている。

Going upstairs from the hallway on the 3rd floor to the lady's changing room. The right side leads to the bedroom and standing and sitting spaces are connected in this composition.

▸ 4階厨房。両脇には、ビルト・インの棚が備え付けられている。使用人の空間もデザインの基調は同じ。

Kitchen on the 4th floor. Built-in shelves are installed on both sides. The design tones are the same for the servants' space too.

▸ 3階洗面室手前の廊下。単調になりがちな天井に幾何学形のデザインが施され、癒しの雰囲気が醸し出される。

Hallway before the toilet on the 3rd floor. Geometrically-designed ceilings create a peaceful atmosphere although ceilings are usually monotonous.

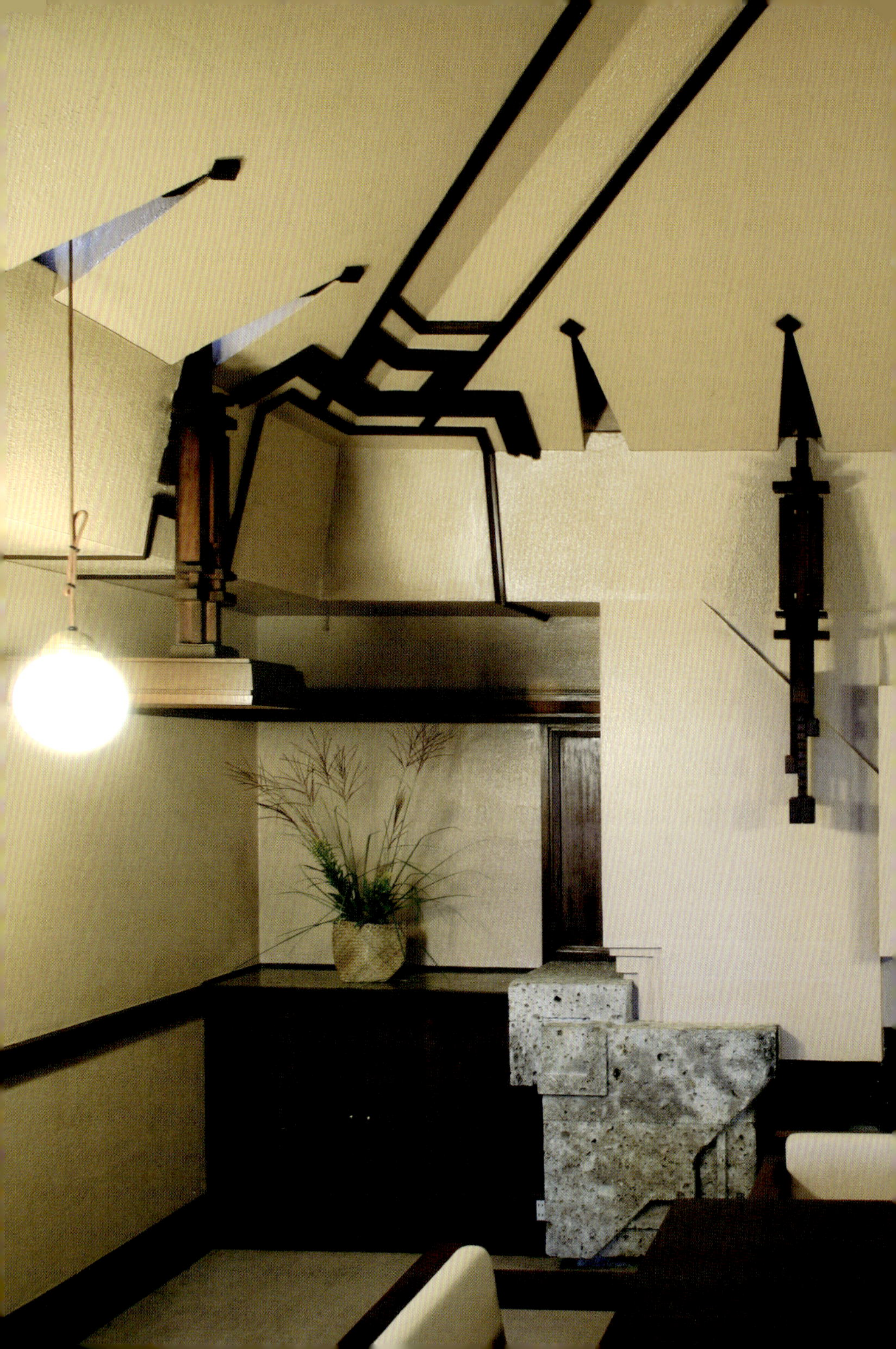

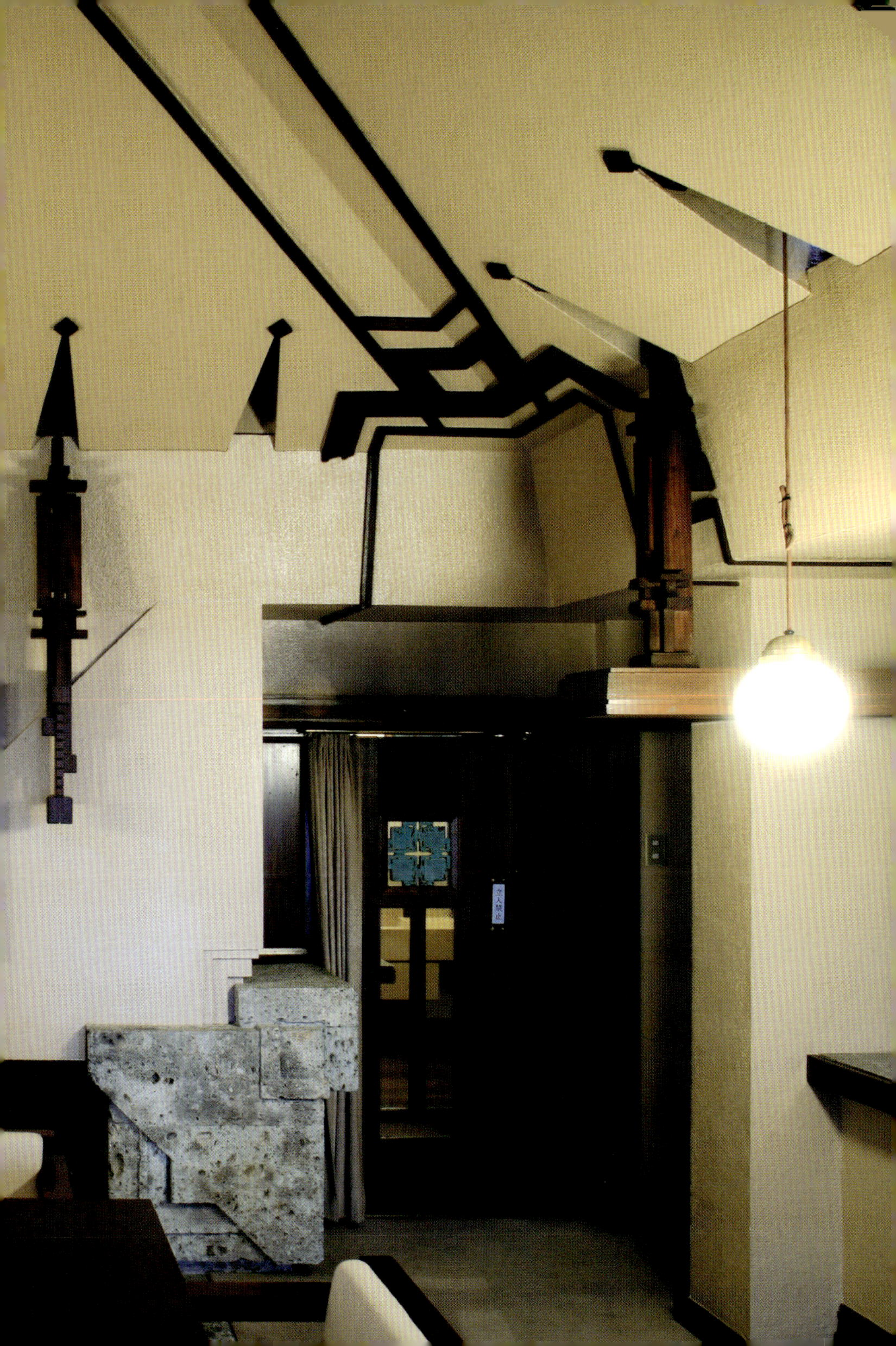
立入禁止

▶ 4階食堂北面。右手扉は、厨房につながる。天井は正四角錐、暖炉を中心に左右対称の厳正なデザイン。食堂は、儀式の空間であるという欧米思想から教会堂内部のような雰囲気がある。

North side of the dining room on the 4th floor. The right side door leads to the kitchen. The ceiling has the shape of a square pyramid and the room is designed symmetrically on either side of the fireplace. This room has a church-like atmosphere because of the Western concept that the dining room is a ritual place.

▶ 天井の小窓に取り付けられた木製飾り。端正でユニークな雰囲気を醸し出している。

Wooden decoration attached to the small windows. They create a clean-cut and unique atmosphere.

▲ 4階食堂、天井が中央部分で最も高くなる船底型になっており、換気口が三角形に仕上げられている。昼間は、ここから光が差し込み、夜間は星空が眺められる。
Dining room on the 4th floor. The ceiling has the shape of a ship's hull with the center part highest. The ventilating holes have a triangular shape. The sunlight penetrates through these holes during the day, and you can see the stars at night.

立面図／Elevation

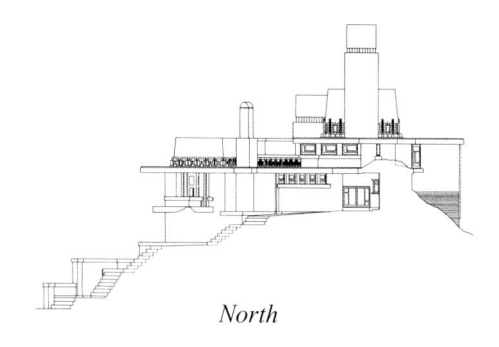

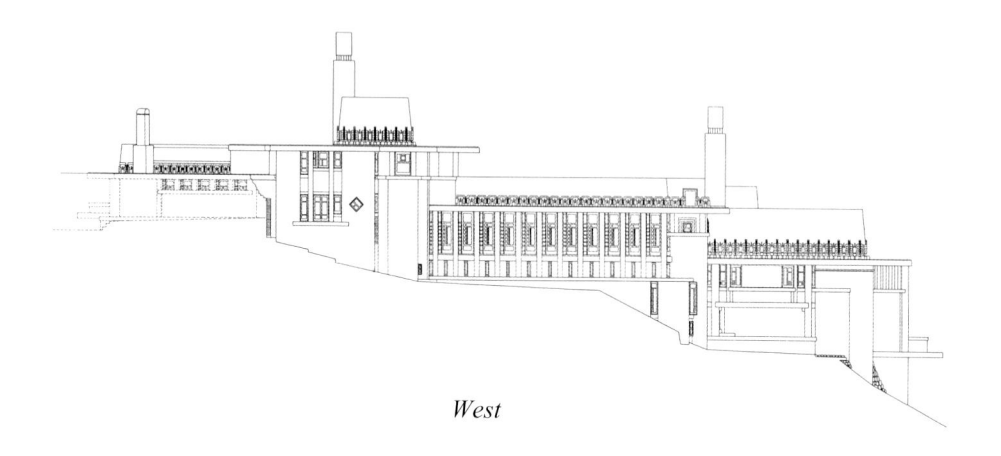

North

West

- 段々畑のように整地され、自然の景観に融け込むように建物が段違いに建てられている。この構想は、ライトの全作品の中でもきわめて特異なもので、芸術性が高い作品といえる。

  The site is prepared like terraced fields and the stair-like buildings blend with the natural landscape. This treatment highly peculiar among all Wright's works and has high artistic quality.

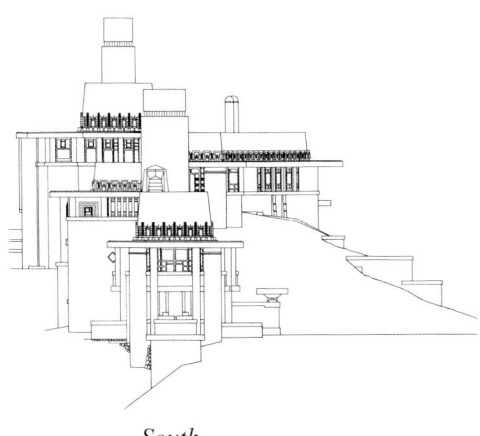

South

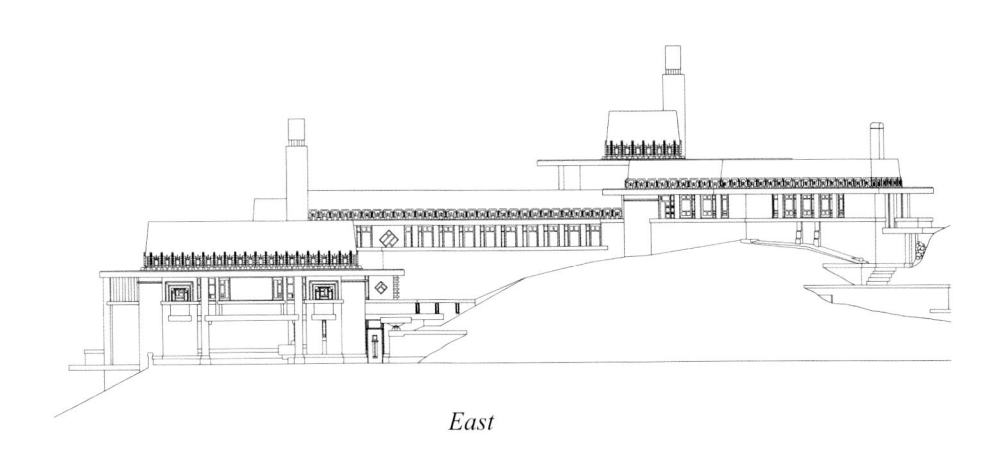

East

旧山邑邸　ヨドコウ迎賓館
建築家：フランク・ロイド・ライト（原設計）
　　　：遠藤新、南信（実施設計）
施工：女良工務店
竣工：1924年
主体構造：鉄筋コンクリート　4階建
敷地面積：約4,700m²
延床面積：約542.43m²
各階面積：1F/37.05m²　2F/164.76m²
　　　　　3F/254.97m²　4F/85.65m²
住所：兵庫県芦屋市山手町173番地
（保存修理工事報告書より）

The Yamamura House (Yodoko Guest House)
Architect: Frank Lloyd Wright (original design)
         : Arata Endo and Makoto Minami (execution design)
Construction: Mera Builder's Office
Completed:1924
Main Structure: Reinforced Concrete, Four Stories
Site Area: about 4,700m²
Total Floor Area: about 542.43m²
Each Floor Area: 1F/37.05m²　2F/164.76m²
　　　　　　　　　3F/254.97m²　4F/85.65m²
Adress:173 Yamatecho Ashiya-shi Hyogo
(Report on Conservation and Repair Work)

▲ 4階食堂から南側へ延びる屋上への出入り口。
Doorway to the rooftop, from the dining room to the south on the 4th floor.

▲ 屋上に張り出した大谷石造りの庇。応接室ベランダの庇と類似した造り。
Eaves made of Oya stone overhanging the rooftop. Similar design to the veranda of the salon.

屋上から4階食堂を望む。庇上部の装飾、延びあがる暖炉の煙突の造形が奥の木々に重なって見える。

Looking at the dining room on the 4th floor from the rooftop. The forms of the decoration on the eaves and the chimney of the fireplace overlap the trees behind.

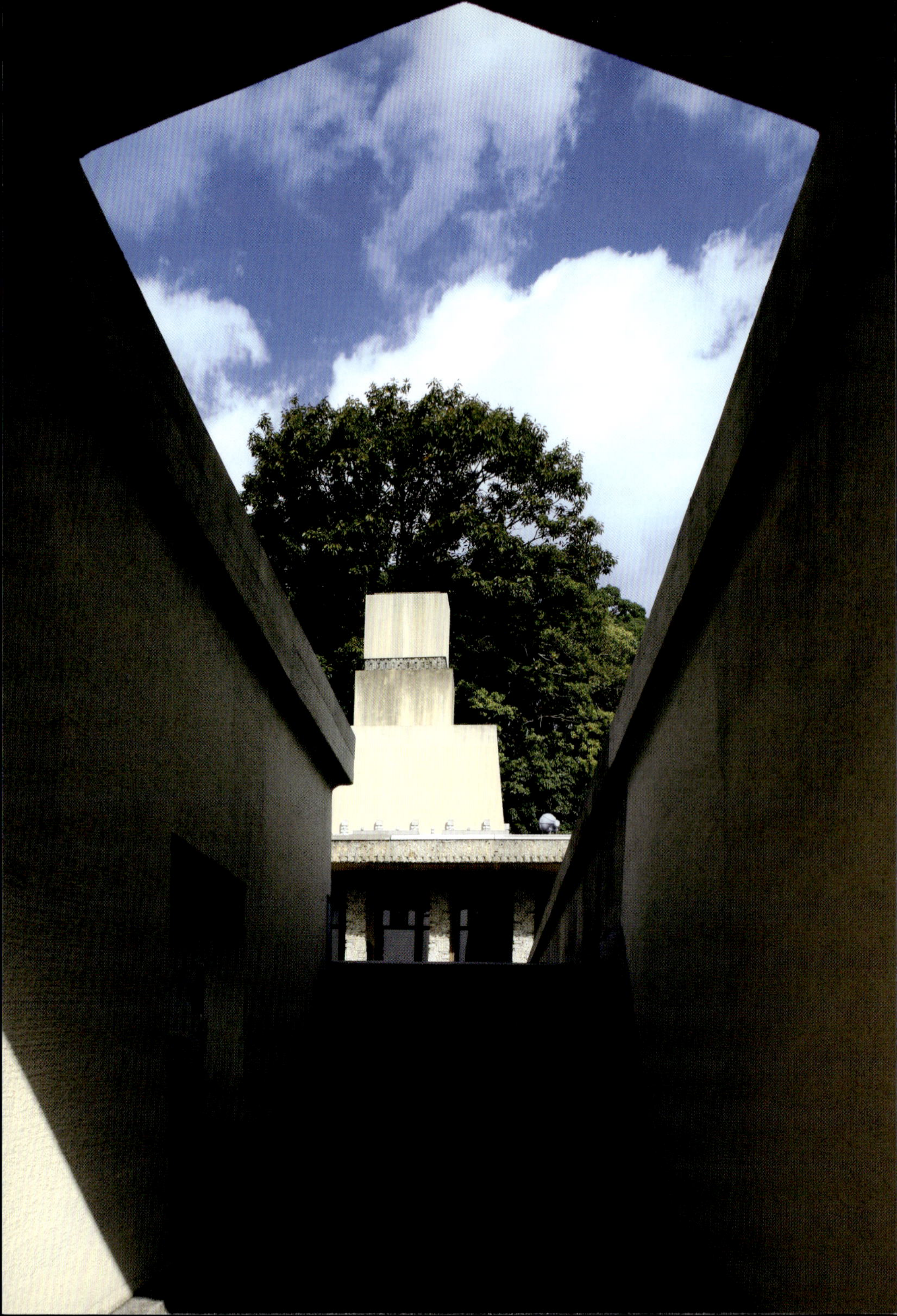

3階屋上と暖炉の煙突。直角の煙突と装飾性豊かな庇のコントラストが軽快感を生む。
Rooftop of the 3rd floor and the chimney of the fireplace. The contrast between the square chimney and the richly decorated eaves creates a feeling of lightness.

◀ 3階屋上から4階食堂を望む。六甲山系の風景との一体感がある。
Looking at the dining room on the 4th floor from the rooftop of the 3rd floor. There is a sense of belonging to the landscape of the Rokko range.

▲ 建物の主軸より30度東に振られた北棟の屋上と4階食堂外観。
Rooftop of the north wing, inclined from the main building axis to the east by 30 degrees, and the appearance of the dining room on the 4th floor.

▲ 玄関前から4階食堂煙突を見上げる。
From the entrance looking up at the 4th floor dining room chimney.

芦屋川から見上げる西南面外観全貌。丘陵の地形に沿って建っていることがよくわかる。

Distant perspective of the southwest appearance from the Ashiya river. You can clearly see that the building follows the shape of the hillside land.

六甲山系の緑滴る茂みの中に融け込んだ全景。

The panoramic landscape of the building integrated with the surrounding greenery of the Rokko range

Detail - 1

外壁を飾るコンクリートの飾石は2種類、いずれも植物の抽象化された幾何学的文様。
上左：寝室ベランダ上部。
上右：食堂上部煙突の脇。
左：応接室の外観、窓廻りや窓台、柱型などすべて大谷石造り。
There are two types of ornamental concrete stone at the outer wall, both of which have abstract geometric botanical patterns.
Above Left: Upper part of the bedroom verandah. Above Right: Beside the chimney on the dining room.
Left: Appearance of the salon. All of the window surrounding parts, window sill and column peripheral parts are made of Oya stone.

2階応接室からベランダに延びる庇と柱。地震の際にかなりの亀裂が入ったり、柱がずれたりした。
Eaves and the column overhanging from the salon to the veranda on the 2nd floor. There were considerable cracks and displacement of columns from the earthquake.

Detail - 2

- 室内に数多く見られる45度傾いた窓。銅板の飾り金物が嵌め込まれている。緑青色の塗色は植物の緑か、吹き出した緑青か。左：和室内西側の壁面にある小窓。他の小窓に比べ一回り大きく、目をひく。右：2階便所上部。

  There are a number of windows angled at 45-degrees. Decorative copper plates are set in the windows. The turquoise color could be of plants or perhaps verdigris. Left: small windows on the west wall of a Japanese-style room. These are slightly larger than other small windows and draw attention. Right: Upper side of the lavatory on the 2nd floor.

- 応接室などに見られる丸グローブブラケット（白熱電灯）。統一されたデザインが飾りバンドにまで施されている。

  Incandescent lights of a spherical shape in the salon etc. Unified design can be seen in the ornamental band.

- 右：3階和室手前の階段脇。真壁造りを思わせる木材の使用。
  下：和室上部の高窓。日本の雨量がライトの想像を上回ったことで通風口として設けられた高窓が、雨仕舞いで問題を起こし、老朽化の一因となった。

Right: The Japanese-style room beside the stairs on the 3rd floor. Usage of timber resembles the half-timber style.
Bottom: High windows of a Japanese-style room. Because the rainfall in Japan exceeded Wright's estimation, these high windows, set as airflow orifices, caused problems of water leakage that partly set in motion the deterioration of the building.

平面図／Floor plans

1st Floor

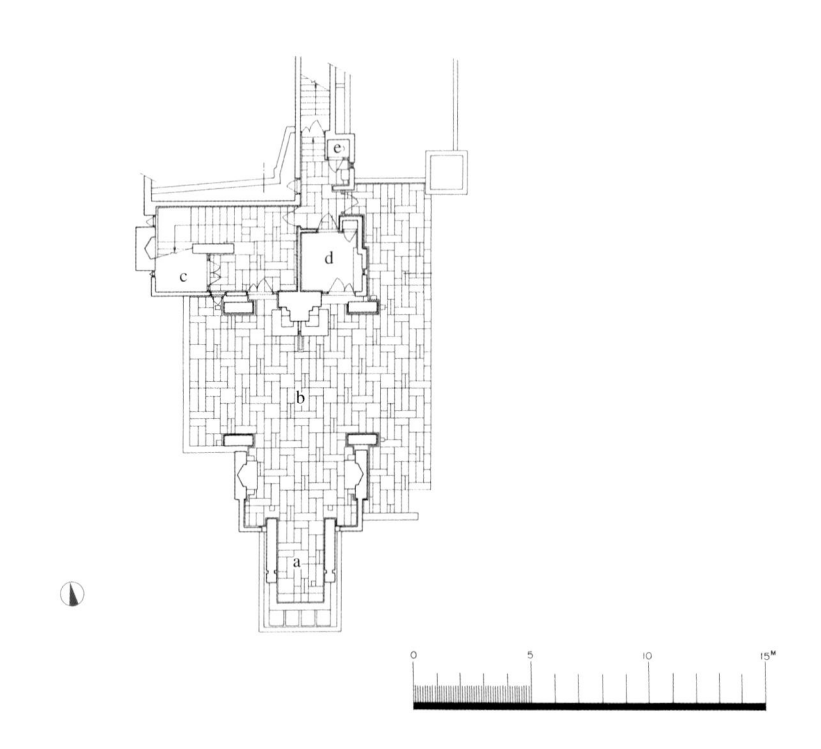

a. ベランダ　b. 車寄　c. 物入　d. クローク　e. 便所
a.Verandah b.Porch c.Storage d.Cloak e.Lavatory

2nd Floor

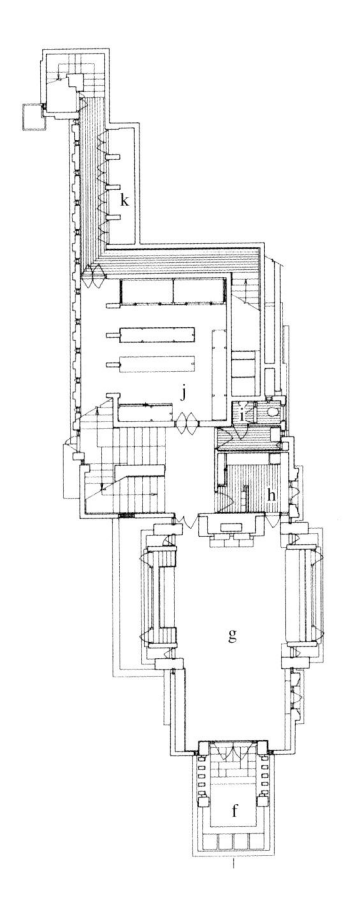

順路に沿って見学できる部分の他、一部に非公開の部分がある。2階応接室の扉と向き合う2枚の鉄扉は、普段閉じられたまま。この先は設備室や倉庫。それを取り巻く廊下がある。下は、玄関裏、上は女中室を経て勝手口に通じている。非公開の部分は別荘番や女中らのサービスのための通路。二つの通路は交錯をさけるよう配慮されている。

There are some areas not open to the public. The two steel doors facing the door to the salon on the 2nd floor usually remain closed. Beyond these steel doors, there is an equipment room and storage. A hallway goes around these rooms. You can go downstairs to the back of the entrance and upstairs will be the kitchen door through the housemaid's room. These private areas are routes for a caretaker of a villa or housemaids. These two routes are carefully located so that they will not cross.

f.バルコニー　g.応接室　h.水屋　i.便所　j.倉庫　k.物入

f.Balcony　g.Salon　h.Service Room　i.Lavatory　j.Storage　k.Storage

3rd Floor

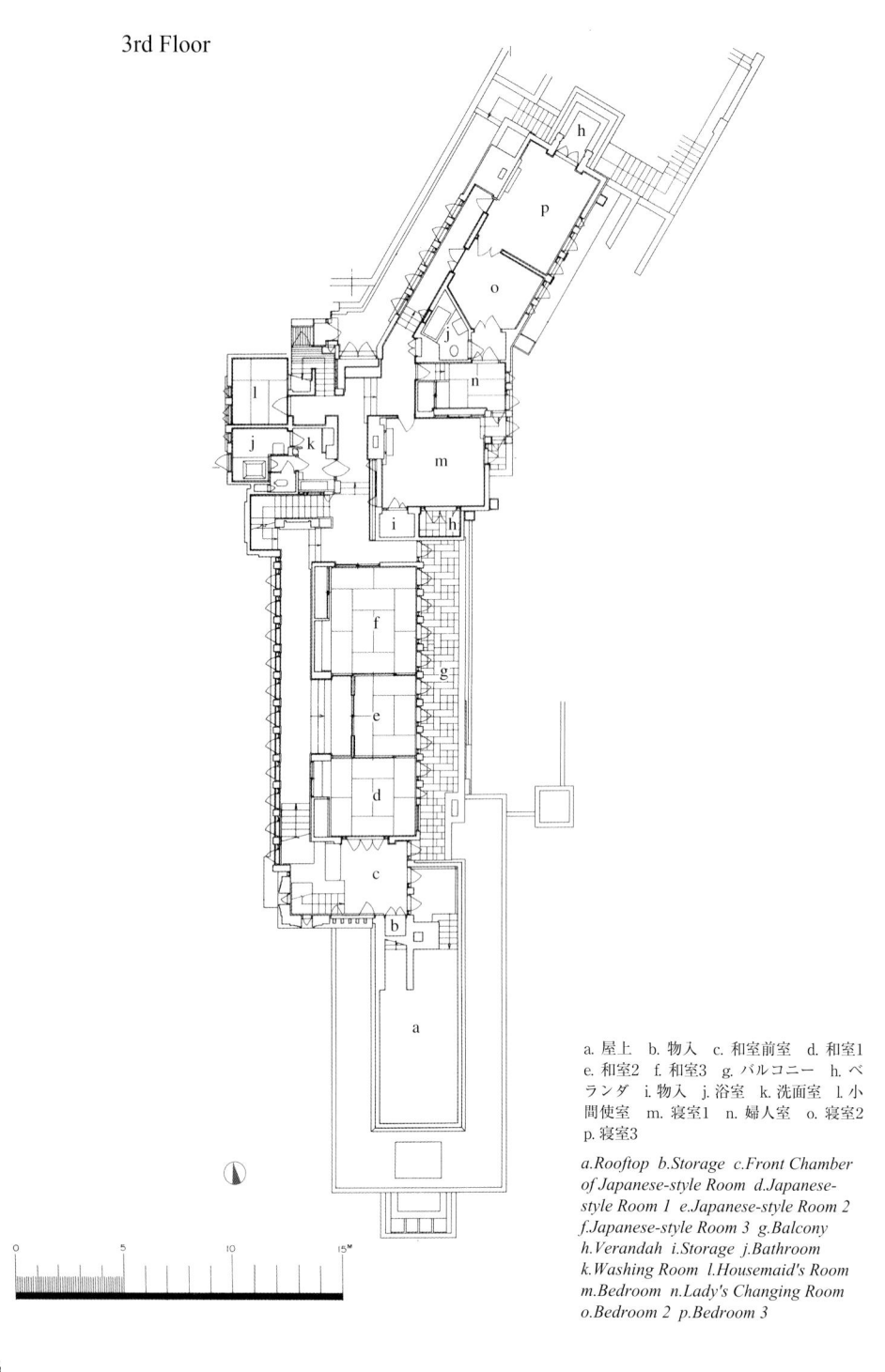

a. 屋上 b. 物入 c. 和室前室 d. 和室1
e. 和室2 f. 和室3 g. バルコニー h. ベランダ i. 物入 j. 浴室 k. 洗面室 l. 小間使室 m. 寝室1 n. 婦人室 o. 寝室2
p. 寝室3

a.Rooftop b.Storage c.Front Chamber of Japanese-style Room d.Japanese-style Room 1 e.Japanese-style Room 2 f.Japanese-style Room 3 g.Balcony h.Verandah i.Storage j.Bathroom k.Washing Room l.Housemaid's Room m.Bedroom n.Lady's Changing Room o.Bedroom 2 p.Bedroom 3

4th Floor

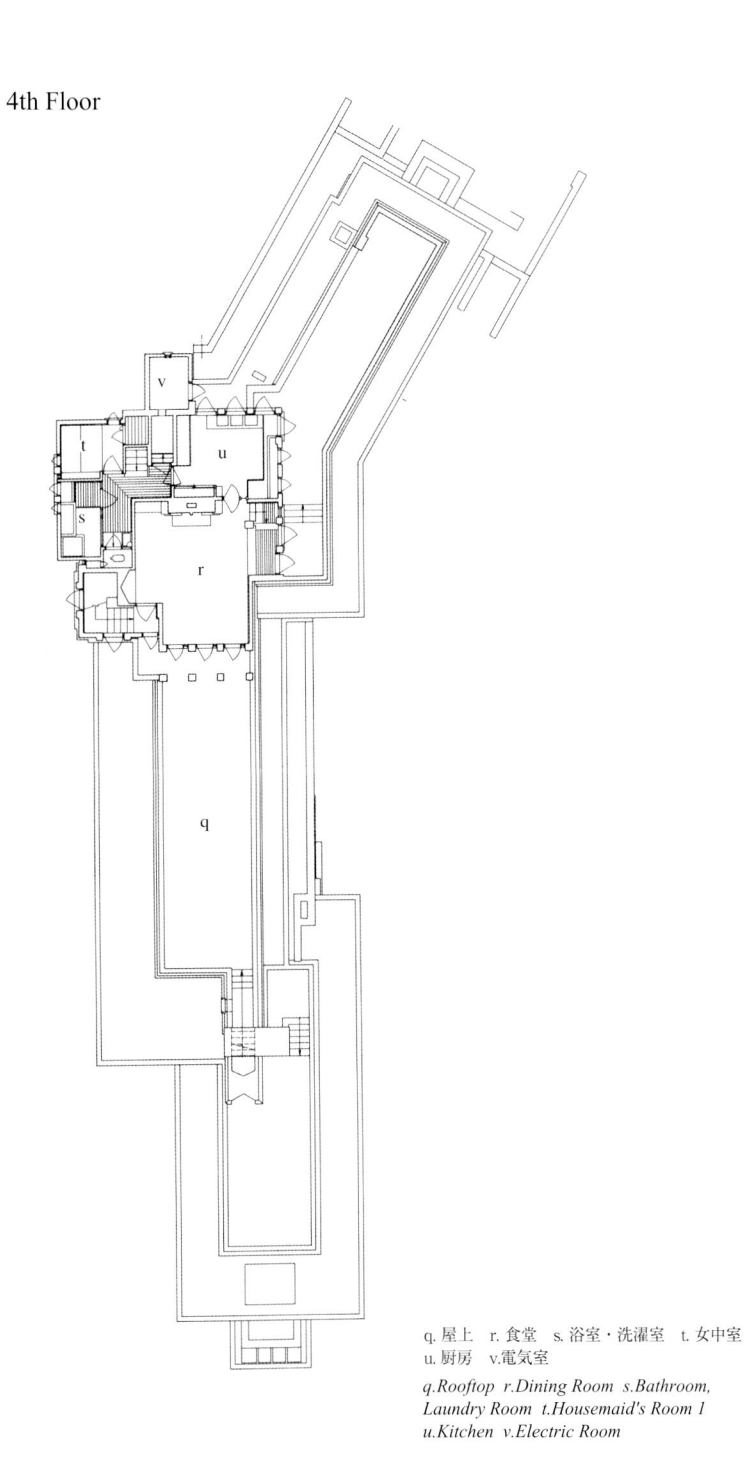

q. 屋上　r. 食堂　s. 浴室・洗濯室　t. 女中室
u. 厨房　v. 電気室

*q.Rooftop r.Dining Room s.Bathroom,
Laundry Room t.Housemaid's Room 1
u.Kitchen v.Electric Room*

生き続ける大谷石住宅の奇跡

電車のホームから望める洋館

　阪急電鉄の梅田駅（大阪）から、神戸線の電車に乗って芦屋川駅で下車。だが、階段を降りて出口へと急がないほうがいい。プラットホームの大阪寄りに行って、ホームと直交して流れる芦屋川の川上に視線を移してほしい。

　六甲山系の山裾の、こんもりとした茂みの間に見え隠れする洋館を望むことができるはずである。洋館といっても格式張った仰々しい建物ではない。大谷石積みを配したコンクリート造のこの洋館は、周囲の緑滴る豊かな自然と融和して穏やかな雰囲気を醸しだしている。不思議なことに、初めて接する人々にさえ親近感を与える建物なのである。阪神間にあって国際文化住宅都市を標榜する芦屋市のほこるべき景観のひとつというべきだろうか。

　この洋館は、アメリカ合衆国が生んだ建築の巨匠フランク・ロイド・ライトが、八代目山邑太左衛門の別邸として、1918年に設計した住宅建築である。

　ライトは、大正年間、帝国ホテル建設のためにわが国に滞在していた。山邑家は、灘の酒造業を営む素封家。別邸の設計をライトに依頼したのは、山邑家の女婿で衆議院議長を務めたこともある星島二郎。彼は、旧制第二高等学校時代の盟友で、ライトの高弟である遠藤新を介して設計依頼を取り付けた。

　設計図が出来上がり、設計料も支払われた旧山邑邸だが、直ぐには工事が始められなかった。ライトが、あの関東大震災の前年の1922年に急遽、帝国ホテルの竣工を見ることなく帰国してしまったからである。山邑家の督促によって、ライトの弟子たちの遠藤新や南信が急ぎ実施設計、施工監理をして1924年にようやく竣工した。

　同邸に畳敷きの和風の部屋があるのは、施主の希望を容れて実施設計時に決定されたことらしい。ライトの原設計に和風の部屋が意図されていたか否かを知る資料はない。

　1972年2月に実測調査をしていた折に発見した棟札には「奉上棟、大正十三年二月十一日、施主　山邑太左衛門、工事設計監理　遠藤新建築創作所、工事施工　女良工務店」とあり、また『新建築』誌第一巻第二号（大正14年9月1日刊）の山邑邸解説、竣工写真、設計図などによって、同邸建設の経緯を詳細に知ることができる。

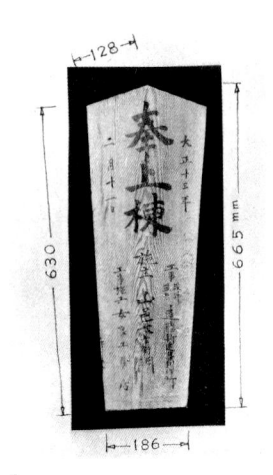

棟札写真。（日本大学工学部　谷川研究室所蔵）
Photo of the Munafuda, a sign staked to a building's ridgepole at construction time (Tanigawa's office, College of Engineering, Nihon University)

The miracle of the surviving Oya Stone House

Western-style building visible from the Train Platform

Take the Hankyu Kobe line from Umeda (Osaka) to Ashiyagawa. But don't rush down the stairs to the exit. Why not walk over to the Osaka side of the platform and take a look at the Ashiya river running beneath the platform?

Hidden among lush growth at the skirts of the Rokko mountain range, you will see a western-style edifice. Although I used the term "edifice," it is not a formal or ostentatious building. This chateau made of reinforced concrete and Oya stone creates a peaceful atmosphere, integrated with the fresh green of the surrounding rich natural environment. Curiously, even someone seeing it for the first time would feel a sense of affinity with this building. This may be one of best views in Ashiya City, which is notable as an international, cultural and residential city of the Hanshin (Osaka-Kobe) area.

Frank Lloyd Wright, the master American architect, designed this building in 1918 as a retreat for Tazaemon Yamamura the 8th.

Wright lived in Japan during the Taisho era for the construction of the Imperial Hotel. The Yamamura family was one of the wealthy sake brewing families of Nada. Jiro Hoshishima, a son-in-law of the Yamamura family who had been the chairman of the Japanese Diet, asked Wright to design a retreat. Hoshishima concluded the contract through the connection of Arata Endo, Wright's disciple as well as Hoshishima's old friend from his days in the former upper school system.

The drawings were completed and the design fee paid for the Yamamura House. However, construction did not start right away because Wright suddenly left Japan in 1922 without seeing the Imperial Hotel completed. The Yamamura family urged Endo and Makoto Minami, Wright's disciples, to proceed with the execution drawings and supervision of work. The Yamamura House was finally completed in 1924.

The house has Japanese-style rooms with tatami flooring. It is said that these rooms were requested by the client at the time the execution drawings were being made. There is no document that tells us whether Wright's original design included these Japanese-style rooms or not.

少壮住宅作家、ライト

　ライトは多作の建築家であった。もっとも、彼は91歳10ヶ月という天寿を全うしたが、1893年、師であるルイス・サリヴァンのもとを去り、独立してから終生70年近い建築家活動によって、400棟を超える作品を遺した。特に1910年までの短期間に、次々と傑作の住宅作品を竣工させて、少壮住宅作家としての地位を不動のものとした。

　シカゴを中心に、合衆国中西部の草原地帯で、大地に根を張り、大地から生え出たような、自然と一体になる、豊かな生活を保障する草原住宅を提供し続けたのだった。

　従来ほとんど指摘されなかったことだが、住宅作家としてのライトが、ホテル建築の大家としてわが国に招聘されるということは、不思議といえば不思議なことである。帝国ホテル建設が目的でわが国を訪れたライトには違いないが、この国に来て住宅をも遺してくれたことはありがたいことである。林愛作邸をはじめ、地震で消滅した福原有信邸、計画案で実現しなかった井上匡四郎子爵邸、さらには帝国ホテルや自由学園、アメリカ大使館計画案までもが、ライトの目指した草原住宅を基底として、合衆国中西部より気象的にも地勢的にも条件の整ったわが国に計画されたり、建設されたことの意義は大きいといえる。

　ところで、旧山邑邸は上記の諸業績とはいささか異質な作品である。

　先に、ライトは多作の建築家だと述べた。だが、コンスタントに仕事があったわけではない。むしろその逆で、多忙を極めた時期とほとんど仕事に恵まれない時期の格差は大きかった。帝国ホテル建設に関わっていた時期は、ライトにとっては不毛、暗黒時代。それでも、ロサンゼルス周辺でいくつかの住宅建設の仕事があった。1917年設計のバーンズダール邸[※1]は、旧山邑邸より一年早く設計された。広いアメリカで、中西部の草原住宅は、亜熱帯地方のロサンゼルスには馴染まない。砂漠の景観とは融和を計るというよりは酷暑から逃れるシェルターが必要と、厚いコンクリート壁の住宅が創案された。この種の住宅は、ライトの全業績のなかでもそれほど多くはない。

　ライトは設計に取りかかる前に、芦屋の旧山邑邸建設予定の敷地に足を運んだ。夜行の急行列車で神戸に着く。朝から太陽の照りつける暑い日。芦屋の背景の六甲山系は、土の見える裸山。これは東京とは違って亜熱帯と理解したのだろうか。ともかく、旧山邑邸はバーンズダール邸と同じ発想で設

[※1] **バーンズダール邸**
ロサンゼルス　1917年、通称：ホリホック・ハウス（立ち葵の家）。中西部に建てられた草原住宅とは異なり、気候風土に対応したシェルター型の住宅。コンクリート・ブロックによる装飾的な造形が特徴。現在は、ロサンゼルス市迎賓館として一般公開。撮影：谷川正己©

[※1] **Barnsdall House**
Los Angeles, 1917
Popular name: Hollyhock House. Different from the Prairie houses in the American Midwest, this house is a shelter-style residence responding to the climate. The decorative form with concrete blocks is characteristic. Currently, this building is open to the public as the guest house of the city of Los Angeles.
Photo: Masami Tanigawa©

● 模型写真。
縮尺1/100、バルサ仕上げ、日本大学工学部　谷川研究室製作（電通・谷川コレクション）
Model photograph.
Scale 1/100, Balsa finishing, Made by Tanigawa's office, College of Engineering, Nihon University, (Tanigawa Collection, Dentsu Inc.)

勝手口への通路は階段を昇降しながら3階まで昇る。
You should climb up the stairs to the 3rd floor to reach the kitchen door.

Wright in his prime as a residential architect

Wright was a notably prolific architect, even if you take it into account his life span of 91 years and 10 months. He designed more than 400 buildings through his nearly 70-year career. He left his mentor Louis Sullivan's office in 1893. Especially during this short period up to 1910, he completed notable homes one after the next. He established an impregnable position as a young residential architect.

Based in Chicago, Wright continued to design prairie houses, in the prairie area of the American Midwest. They appeared to be rooted into and growing out of the ground, guaranteeing a rich life with nature.

It has seldom been pointed out how strange it was that a residential architect like Wright was invited to Japan as an authority on hotel architecture. Certainly he came for the purpose of designing the Imperial Hotel, but fortunately he designed residences as well. His works from that period include the house of Aisaku Hayashi, the house of Arinobu Fukuhara that was demolished by the earthquake, the house of Viscount Tadashiro Inoue which was never built, the Imperial Hotel, the Jiyu Gakuen School and a proposed plan for the American Embassy. It is significant that these were designed based upon the "Prairie House", but in Japan, which enjoys more favorable climactic and geographical conditions than the American Midwest.

However, the Yamamura House differs from the works described above.

I noted previously that Wright was a prolific architect. However, he did not have constant work. On the contrary, there was a big gap between the times when his business was good and bad. It was a dark period for Wright when he was involved with the construction of the Imperial Hotel. He had some residential projects in the Los Angeles area. The Barnsdall House[*1] (1917) was designed one year earlier than the Yamamura House. In the USA, with its diverse climates, the Prairie House of the Midwest was not suitable for subtropical Los Angeles. Therefore, a house built with thick concrete walls was invented to escape from the intense heat of the desert, instead of integrating with the landscape. You cannot find many residences of this kind among all Wright's works.

Wright visited the planned construction site for the Yamamura House in Ashiya before designing the house. An overnight express took him to Kobe. The naked soil of the Rokko mountains formed the backdrop to the Ashiya landscape, with the burning sun. He might have regarded this area as subtropical and different from

計された。わが国での草原住宅として建設された住宅とは異質の貴重な遺産ということになる。

文化財指定へ

　旧山邑邸は、1935年には、人手に渡り、別荘や事務所として使用された。戦後は一時期進駐軍の社交場となったこともある。（株）淀川製鋼所の所有となったのは、1947年のこと。同社はこの建物を社長住宅、貸家、社員寮などとして使用した。その後、1974年5月に国の重要文化財建造物に指定され、これを契機に淀川製鋼迎賓館（略称：ヨドコウ迎賓館）と呼ばれることになった。

　竣工後わずか50年で文化財としての建築の価値が認められ、大正期の建築の指定第1号となった。官報の文部省告示第七十九号に原設計ライト、実施設計遠藤新、南信と記されている。

旧山邑邸の特徴

アプローチ

　建物の敷地の西側を芦屋川が流れている。東側は六甲山系を山越えして有馬温泉に至る芦有道路の出発点にあたり、南北に細長い南斜面の台地の突端部が敷地である。西および南側は急峻な崖地。道路からのアプローチは北側。そして、建物の玄関は敷地の最奥部南端に用意されている。建物の内部に入る以前から、ユニークでドラマチックな構成である。敷地の選定をしたのは山邑家なのだが、この建物に至る導入部のドラマは、あの阪急電鉄のプラットホームから始まっている。

　茂みの間に見える建物の全容は、芦屋川沿いの道路を歩いて川上へと進むと、いよいよ大きく見えてきて、期待に胸が膨らむ。丁度カメラのファインダーを覗いて、ズーミングをしているようだ。芦屋川に架かる開森橋を渡って左折すると、路傍の「ライト坂」と記された銘板に出会う。近隣の市民の命名だという。勾配の厳しい坂道を登って入口に到達する。この住宅は巨体だが、圧迫感はない。右手に見える建物の東側外観を詳細に鑑賞しながら、ようやく玄関に到着する。こうしたアプローチはわが国ではあまり見かけない手法であり、

建物最南端。2階バルコニーから芦屋市が一望できる。

South end of the building. You can have a full view of Ashiya city from the balcony on the 2nd floor.

Tokyo. At any rate, the Yamamura House was designed with the same concept as the Barnsdall House. The residence represents a significant heritage that is distinctive from the Prairie Houses that were built in Japan.

Designation as a Cultural Property

The Yamamura house passed into others' hands and was used as a second home or office. It was also once used as an officers' club place for the occupation forces after the war. In 1947, the house became the property of Yodogawa Steel Works, Ltd., and at first the company used it as an official residence for the corporate president, then as a rental property and an apartment for employees. The house was later designated a National Important Cultural Property, which prompted its name to be changed to "Yodoko Guest House."

Only 50 years after the completion of the house, it was designated a Cultural Property. It was the first such designation during the Taisho era. The announcement of this designation by the Ministry of Education in Report No. 79 noted that the original designer was Frank Lloyd Wright and the execution designers were Arata Endo and Makoto Minami.

Features of the Yamamura House

Approach

The Ashiya river runs through the site on the west side. The east side is the starting point of the Royu Driveway, which leads through the Rokko range to the Arima hot springs. The site itself occupies a long and thin stretch of land running north to south at the headland of a south-sloping plateau. The west and south sides are precipitous cliffs. You approach the site from the north and enter from the opposite end at the south. This approach creates a unique and dramatic visual composition even before reaching the building. Although the Yamamura family selected this site, the drama towards the building starts at that platform of the Hankyu train.

Approaching the building walking upstream along the Ashiya river, it grows larger amongst the luxuriant growth just as if one were zooming in on it through the viewfinder of a camera. Then you will see the sign that says "Wright slope," which is the name given to it by its neighbors. This steep slope takes you to the site. Although this residence is huge, the feeling is not oppressive.

欧米的なものというべきだろうか。例えが大袈裟になってはしまうが、アテネのアクロポリスの丘に建つパルテノン神殿は、プロピレイアを潜り抜けた右手前方に姿を表す。それは同神殿の背面である。正面に至るためには、同神殿の側面態を鑑賞しながらプロピレイアより最も遠い位置まで歩かなければならない。旧山邑邸へのアプローチはこれに似ている。

大谷石

　建物の外観はコンクリートの壁面と大谷石を使用している。大谷石は帝国ホテルで多用されていた石材であることは周知の通りである。帝国ホテルの建設工事中に、わが国の国会議事堂の建設工事も進んでいた。建築材料はすべて国産品であることという規制があって、大蔵省臨時建築局には国内産石材標本室があった。この情報を得たライトは、標本室を訪ねて石材を選定した。石川県産の通称「蜂ノ巣石」と呼ばれる菩提石を希求する。那谷寺で知られる同県江沼郡那谷村（現：小松市那谷町）で産出する菩提石は産出量が少なく、ライトの希求を満たすことができないとわかる。再び、標本室を訪ねたライトは、性質の類似した栃木県宇都宮市近郊産の大谷石に切り替える。菩提石は、赤味を帯びた暖色系、大谷石は青味を帯びた寒色系。ライトが、この石材の変更に不満であったか否かを知る文献は遺されてはいない。
　ライトは帝国ホテルのみならず、彼のわが国での業績のほとんどすべてに大谷石を使用して、彼の個性的な建物の相貌としたかったのだろうか。大谷石を老舗の石材店から購入せず、ホテル直営の「東谷石材商会」を設立させて、帝国ホテル建設現場での需要を満たした。
　実は、旧山邑邸の建設予定の敷地にも、ライトが帰国する以前に運び込まれていたようで、この建物でも大谷石によって彼の特徴となる外観に仕上げられる予定になっていた。帝国ホテルほど多量にというわけではないが、旧山邑邸で軒庇先、開口部廻り、壁頂部、腰壁および柱型に大谷石が用いられ、豊穣な雰囲気を演出している。長いアプローチの末の、玄関部分は、車寄せの床をはじめ、2階の窓廻り、柱型、腰壁、大きな花鉢にいたるまで、幾何学的な凹凸の施された大谷石によって装飾されている。室内に入る以前に、賓客を昂揚させる演出が整えられている。

Appreciating the details of the east aspect of the building to your right, one finally reaches the entrance. This kind of approach, not often seen in Japan, could perhaps be called Western. Although this may be overstating it a bit, but for example, the Parthenon in Acropolis, Athens appears to your right after you pass through the Propylaia gate. You will see the back of the Parthenon first and must walk beyond the Propylaia to face the front façade of the Parthenon at last. The approach to the Yamamura House is similar to this.

Oya Stone

The outside of the house is made of concrete walls and Oya stone. It is well known that Oya stone was used heavily for the Imperial Hotel. During the construction of the Hotel, the Diet Building of Japan was also being constructed. At the time, there was a regulation that all the architectural materials for the building should be domestic, so therefore, they created a temporary architectural bureau at the finance department. The bureau had a room contain samples of domestic stone materials. Hearing about this, Wright visited this room to select stone materials. He desired a kind of stone from Ishikawa prefecture, which is called "honeycomb stone." However, Wright came to know that the output of this stone is low and would not satisfy his needs. He again visited the sample room to pick up Oya stone, which has similar characteristics and originates from the area around Utsunomiya city, Tochigi prefecture. Honeycomb stone has a reddish warm color, while Oya stone a bluish cold color. We cannot discern from the documents whether or not Wright was satisfied with this change of stone.

Wright utilized Oya stone not only for the Imperial Hotel, but also for almost all his achievements in Japan. He might have hoped that the stone would be a symbol for his distinctive buildings. He did not buy Oya stone from well-established stone material companies, but established a firm "To-o-ya" to supply Oya stone and send directly to the hotel construction site.

Oya stone was brought to the planned construction site for the Yamamura House before Wright left Japan. It was intended that the building would have a Wright-like appearance with the stone. Although not so much as the Imperial Hotel, Oya stone is utilized for eaves, openings, wall-tops, window backs and column peripheral parts of the residence to create a fertile atmosphere. At the end of a long approach, the entrance is fully decorated with geometrically-engraved Oya stone; from the driveway to the windows on the 2nd floor, columns, sills and even a large flower pot. Thus the stage is set for visiting guests even before entering the building.

断面形の妙味

　旧山邑邸の平面図は4枚必要。つまり、4階建てというわけだが、いくつかの階段を登って4階の食堂や広い屋上に到達しても、ほとんど疲労を覚えない。この建物の妙味は、断面形にある。丘陵地の自然と一体化を計るために、棚田あるいは段々畑の要領で整地されている。断面図を見れば2階以上に階を重ねる部分は無いのだが、平面図が4枚になるという、きわめて革新的な構成に仕上げられている。つまり、それぞれの部屋で視点の位置が異なり、違った開口部からの景観が堪能できるというわけである。先に旧山邑邸より一年早い業績である、ロサンゼルスに建つバーンズダール邸との類似性について触れたが、バーンズダール邸は丘の頂部を平坦に整地して建てられているから、単純に比較はできないが、旧山邑邸の敷地との関わり方のユニークな構成は見事である。

　ライトは1911年以降、彼の住居兼設計事務所をウィスコンシン州のスプリング・グリーンに建設、この根拠地をウェールズ語の「タリアセン[*2]（Taliesin）」と命名した。これは、ウェールズのアーサー王物語に登場する騎士の名前でもあるのだが、英語では「輝ける額（shining brow）」。ライトは「背景となる丘の稜線に建物を建ててはいけない。常に山懐に（丁度、顔の額に当たる部分に）点々と建物を建てて、自然と融和しなければならない。そして、額にあたる部分に建てられた建物はキラキラと輝き、周辺の自然さえもが光彩を放つのだ」と解説して、それを実現した。尊大とも取れる解説だが、彼の建築家としての自信を覗かせる。

　仕事に恵まれなかった時代にあたるライトのわが国での業績は、それ故にそれぞれに精力的に取り組むことで傑作が生み出された、といえるのではないだろうか。

[*2] タリアセン
1911年、ウィスコンシン州スプリング・グリーンに建設された、ライトの自邸と設計事務所。現在みられる建築群は、二度の火災で焼失後1925年以降に建設されたもの。なだらかな丘の中腹に点々と建つ自邸、スタッフの宿舎、農場倉庫、設計事務所は自然と一体化して輝く景観を醸し出している。
撮影：谷川正己©

[*2] *Taliesin*
Wright's own house and architectural office in Spring Green, Wisconsin in 1911. The buildings you can see now are the ones reconstructed in 1925 after two disastrous fires. Brightly combined with nature are a residence, a staff house, a barn and an architectural office across the gently sloping hill.
Photo: Masami Tanigawa©

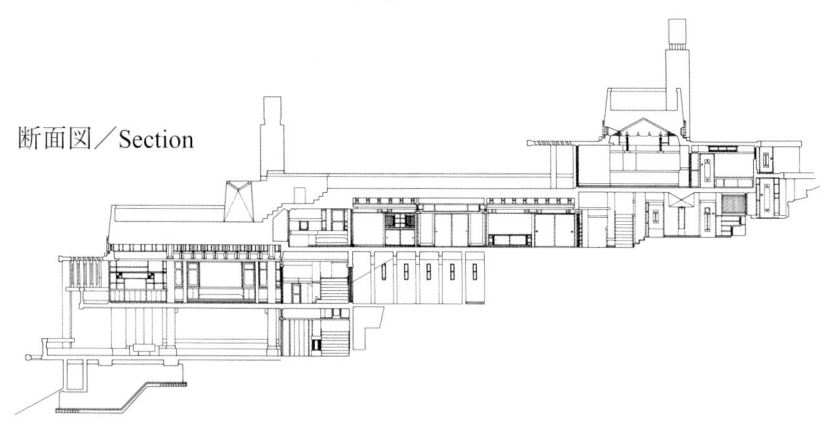

断面図／Section

The charm of the cross-section

The Yamamura House needs four floor plans, in other words, it is a four story building. But you will hardly feel tired even after climbing the stairs to reach the dining room or large rooftop on the 4th floor. The charm of this building is embedded in its cross-section shape. The site was terraced in order to harmonize the building with hilly surroundings. Another innovative concept is that there is no overlapping of more than 2 floors although there are 4 floors. This is so you can enjoy different views from different rooms. The Yamamura House utilizes a unique composition in its relationship to the site. For example, the previously mentioned Barnsdall House (built one year earlier in Los Angeles), shows some similarities, and is located on a flat site on a hill.

In 1911, Wright built his own house and architectural office in Spring Green, Wisconsin. He named this new base in Welsh, "Taliesin[*2]". This is the name of a warrior in the legends of King Arthur, and means "shining brow" in English. Wright said "there should not be any buildings on the ridge line of the background hill. We should locate buildings around the middle of the mountains, like the brow on the face. In this way, we can integrate with nature. The buildings on the brow will shine brightly and so will the surrounding natural environment." He realized such concepts. This manifesto might sound arrogant, but we see in it a hint of his confidence as an architect.

Perhaps Wright's achievements in Japan created just when his career was faltering, are such masterpieces because had to tackle them with all the vigor he could command.

実測をしていて解ったことだが、この和洋折衷の住宅では用尺が2種類ある。外観に関わる部分はヤード・ポンド法のスケール、内部は尺貫法のスケールで設計されているらしい。外壁にわずかな息角があるため、壁厚は上部に向かって薄くなっていて、2種類の用尺を壁厚で調整している。(日本大学工学部 谷川研究室所蔵 原設計図トレース図面)

It was revealed at the measurement survey that there are 2 types of measurements adapted for this residence as a compromise between East and West. The yard-pound system is used for the portions regarding outside appearance, and the Japanese measuring system for the interior. Because there is slight repose angle to the outer walls, the thickness of the wall lessens towards the top. Thus, 2 types of measurement are adjusted by the thickness of the wall.
(Traced drawing of the original drawing, collection of Tanigawa's office, College of Engineering, Nihon University)

3階平面図／3rd Floor Plan

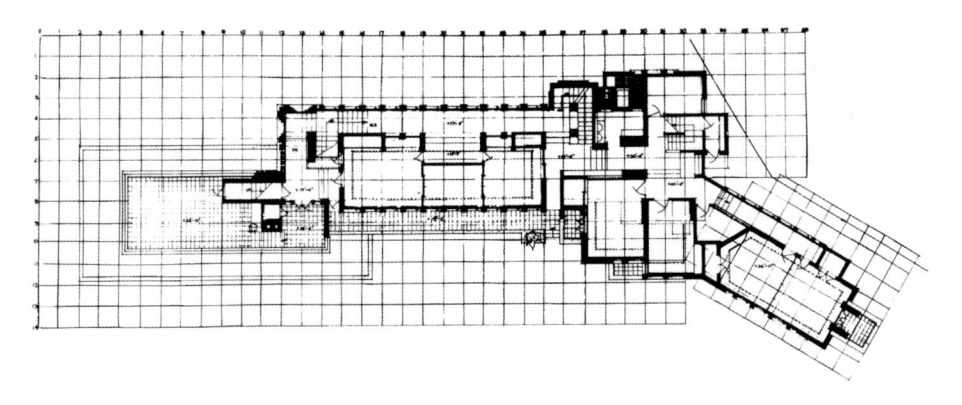

ライトが受けた日本建築の影響

　それぞれの部屋の天井は段差のある二重の天井。周囲の低い天井と、一段高い中央部の天井は、わが国の折り上げ天井を連想させる。折り上げ天井は、本来部屋の格付けに由来するものだが、ライトは低い天井によって建物の高さを抑え、高い天井によってより広い部屋を実現した。段差の部分は、設備のスペースとして使い、ここに小さい開口部を用意して、湿気の多いわが国の通風換気に配慮する設計をした。

　各部屋に数多く備えられた収納スペースは本来はわが国特有の設備であった。押し入れや物入れ、書棚などのビルト・インは、限られたスペースの有効利用であり、先人たちの生活の知恵として伝承されてきた。欧米にあっては、部屋は壁で囲まれた空間、そこに家具が運び込まれて生活が始まるというのが基本である。ライトは、わが国にきてこのビルト・インに着目し、積極的にこれを採用した。

　わが国の真壁造り（柱や梁より薄い壁というのが原則）の柱や梁のストラクチュアの露出が、そのままインテリアとして室内に生気を与える点、あるいは装飾として付加される長押の美的効果に関心をもったライトは、インテリアに木材を多用して、美的な造形を実現しているなど、多くの日本の影響が指摘できる。

　ライトは終生、「わたしの作品にみられる日本の建築や美術の影響を、すべて否定する」といっていた。多分、これらの指摘も一蹴されそうだが、芸術が庶民の間に溢れている日本に敬意を表して、われわれへの贈り物として旧山邑邸を設計したのだろうと思う。少なくとも欧米的発想とは異なる設計指針を基底としているが故に、この建物に親近感を持つのである。

重要文化財、旧山邑邸

旧山邑邸が救われた

　旧山邑邸にも危機があった。1971年秋、同邸が取壊されて跡地にマンションが建設されるらしいという情報が流れた。日本建築学会の大会が関西大学で開催されていた折りである。建築史研究関係者の有志が急遽集まり、同邸の所有者である淀川製鋼所をはじめ、兵庫県、芦屋市などに保存の要望書を作成、提出した。あの帝国ホテル保存運動が功を奏することなく消滅して、3年半ばかり後のことだったが、再び同じ結末

The influence of Japanese Architecture on Wright

The rooms have tray ceilings; the peripheral space being and the central space higher, which reminds us of the Oriage ceiling in Japan. Although the Oriage ceiling originates with room ratings, Wright used this technique to balance the lower height of the building outside and the high-ceilinged spacious rooms inside. The stepped portion on the periphery of the ceiling is utilized for equipment and Wright designed small openings in them to allow for ventilation in Japan's humid climate.

A number of storage spaces in each room are essentially distinctive to Japan. The built-in style for closets, storage and bookshelves is an efficient use of limited space and is part of Japan's traditional wisdom of daily life that has been passed down through the generations. In Western culture, a room is a walled space and your life basically starts with furniture brought in. Wright paid attention to this built-in style in Japan and utilized it without hesitation.

You can easily point out Japanese influence on Wright's architecture such as realizing aesthetic forms with the heavy use of wood material indoors. He was interested in the exposure of columns and beams as interior parts giving vitality or ornamental effects of Nageshi, decorative beams.

Throughout his life, Wright constantly said, "I deny all influence of Japanese architecture or art on my works." This statement may be dismissed, but he may have designed the Yamamura House as a gift for us to show his respect to Japan, where art is popular among ordinary people. At least one of the reasons for the attractiveness of this building is that it is designed with different planning policies than used in the West.

Important Cultural Property, the Yamamura House

Saving the Yamamura House

The Yamamura House was once in danger. There was news in fall, 1971 that the house would be destroyed and an apartment building would be built there. At this time, the annual meeting of Architectural Institute of Japan (AIJ) was being held at Kansai University. Architectural historians and others gathered promptly to write and submit a request to the Yodogawa Steel Works, Ltd., owner of the house, as well as Hyogo prefecture and Ashiya city to

を迎えてはならないと思った。建築学会近畿支部には「旧山邑邸保存に関する特別委員会」が設置されて、帝国ホテルのように知名度が高くない同邸の価値を、一般の人々にも知らせようと『旧山邑邸理解のために』という小冊子を作成した。いや、一般の人々はもちろん、建築界でも同邸を知る人はほとんどいなかった。この旧山邑邸の価値を再認識しようと、シンポジウムなども行われた。実は、マンション建設計画は設計図も出来上がり、更にその模型も完成していた。私たちは、所有者からの連絡をひたすら待った。3年あまり経った1974年春になって、同社から「社長が今一度山邑邸の価値について伺いたいということなので、ご足労願いたい」との連絡があった。

私はこの時、特別委員会の人々に「淀川製鋼所の社長さんは一人しかおられない。こちらからも伺って説明するのは一人で充分だ。私に行かせて欲しい」と持論を吐露して、これを了承してもらった。複数人で伺うことは、所有者に圧力を掛けること、断じてやってはならないことという思いがあった。保存を希求する者と所有者が敵対する形で、期待する回答を得られるはずがない、と信じていた。1974年4月3日、当時の社長井上利行氏に会うために、私は一人で同社を訪問した。社長室では、総務部長、開発部長、広報課長も同席された。30分と短い時間ではあったが、旧山邑邸の価値についての説明を終えた。次の瞬間、井上社長がこのように述べられた。「解りました。マンション建設計画は撤回しましょう。文化財指定を願い出るために、この建物の価値について推薦文を書いていただけますか」。正に鶴の一声であり、私は社長の依頼を快諾した。何より嬉しかったのは、井上社長が同邸に愛情を示されたことであった。

二冊ある修理報告書

重要文化財に指定された「旧山邑家住宅（淀川製鋼迎賓館）」の保存修理の報告書は2冊ある。第1冊は、保存修理工事報告書（平成元年 [1989年] 2月刊）、第2冊目は、保存修理災害復旧工事報告書（平成10年 [1998年] 3月刊）。わずか10年の間に2度も修理工事が行われたということである。

具体的にいうと、第1冊は1974年に重要文化財に指定された旧山邑邸も、建設以来60余年経過し建物各部の腐朽、破損が目立ってきたため、1985年7月から1988年10月まで3年3ヶ月の工期で修理をした報告書である。

● 南東ジャッキアップ施工状況。
Southeast jack-up construction.

conserve the building. The request stated their hope that this building would not suffer the same fate as the Imperial Hotel, which disappeared regardless of their efforts to preserve it. We established a "Special Committee on the Conservation of the former Yamamura House" at the AIJ Kinki Branch, and created a pamphlet entitled "Understanding the former Yamamura House" to make known to the public the building's value, which was not as popular as the Imperial Hotel. Even most people in the architectural world did not know about this house. There were also symposiums held to re-acknowledge the worth of the Yamamura house. However, the drawings were finished and the model completed for the proposed apartment building. In the meanwhile, the group continued to wait patiently for a reply to their request for preservation. In spring 1974, about 3 years later, we received a message saying "we would like to invite you to our office because the president would like to be briefed on the worth of the Yamamura House again."

I said to the members of our committee to preserve the house, "There is only one president of Yodogawa Steel. So one person should be enough to talk to them. Please let me be that one." They agreed. I was thinking that we should never visit there in a group because it would pressure the owner. I was sure that we could not expect a good response if we seemed antagonistic. I visited the company to meet then president Mr. Toshiyuki Inoue on 3rd April, 1974. Also present at the meeting in the president's office were the administrative manager, the development manager and the PR section chief. I finished my explanation of the worth of the Yamamura House in half an hour. In the next moment, president Inoue said, "I understand. We will withdraw our plan to build the apartment. Would you write a recommendation letter about the value of this residence in order to apply for designation as a Cultural Property?" It was quite a request receive from the top and I gave my ready consent. The most pleased me, was that President Inoue showed his love for this house.

2階応接室内部雑作解体状況。
Demolition work of interior decorating of the salon on the 2nd floor.

Two Repair Reports

There are two repair reports on the "former Yamamura House (Yodoko Guest House)," which was designated as an Important Cultural Property. The first one is the repair construction report (February, 1989), and the second is the disaster recovery report (March, 1998). During only 10 years, repairs performed on the house twice.

The first report covers restoration carried out over a period of 3

第2冊は、1995年1月17日未明に発生した阪神大震災で被災した同邸が、再び修理工事を余儀なくされ、1995年6月から1998年3月まで2年9ヶ月の工期で修理をした報告書である。
　見方によれば、旧山邑邸は幸運に恵まれて、10年ばかりの間に二度も修復されたということかもしれない。しかし、最初の修理工事の前に、調査工事が9ヶ月も費やして行われ、修理工事開始後にも、更に車寄せ廻りの基礎の不具合を追加工事で修理しながら、地震の被害を喰い止められなかったことを残念に思う。

保存意識の困難を克服して

　旧山邑邸の二度目の修理工事（災害復旧工事）は、迅速で的確なものであった。被災した同邸の修復はもちろん、新たな基礎を加えて耐震補強の工事も実施された。文化財行政の確かさを見せつけられた思いがする。
　最初の修理工事費が総額2億3500万円（国庫補助50％、兵庫県補助15％、芦屋市補助15％、所有者負担20％）であったのに対して、災害復旧工事費は、総額5億4000万円余（国庫補助70％、兵庫県補助10％、芦屋市補助10％、震災復旧基金補助5％、所有者負担5％）の巨費が投じられた。
　そもそも、わが国と欧米とでは、建物の寿命についての概念は根本的に異なっていた。石や煉瓦で築き上げられた建物は、原則的に壊れない。震害や火災に遭遇しなければ、未来永劫に建ち続けるものと思われてきた。わが国の場合、江戸期以前は木と紙で組み立てられた建物。震害や火害に遭遇しなくても、やがて朽ち果てるものと理解されてきた。火災が

ライトの日本での設計業績

1　帝国ホテル、東京、1912年
2　アメリカ大使館、東京、1914年
3　林愛作邸、東京、1917年
4　小田原ホテル、小田原、1917年
5　福原有信邸、箱根、1918年
6　井上匡四郎子爵邸、東京、1918年
7　三原邸、東京、1918年
8　映画劇場、東京、1918年
9　山邑太左衛門邸、芦屋、1918年
10　帝国ホテル別館、東京、1920年
11　後藤新平男爵邸、東京、1921年
12　自由学園、東京、1921年

他に、執行弘道邸、日比谷三角ビルディング、総理官邸など数が増える可能性がある。
ライトの国外での業績は、計画案を含めてわずか32件以上、うち日本での業績は12件以上。実現した作品数となると、日本で6、カナダで3、計9件しかない。
現存するライトの国外の作品は、日本に4件（帝国ホテル、林愛作邸、旧山邑邸、自由学園明日館）しかなく旧山邑邸がいかに貴重であるかがわかる。

帝国ホテル
東京、1912年。日比谷公園と道路を隔てて建っていた帝国ホテルは、1968年老朽化を理由に消滅したが、大谷石とスクラッチ煉瓦で特色ある容姿を誇るわが国第一級のホテルとして親しまれてきた。装飾の溢れる傑作。現在は、愛知県犬山市にある野外博物館「明治村」に玄関回りからロビー周辺の一部が再現保存されている。撮影：谷川正己©

The Imperial Hotel
Tokyo, 1912. The Imperial Hotel standing across the street from Hibiya Park disappeared due to deterioration of the building in 1968. The Hotel was popular as one of Japan's greatest hotels with its distinctive appearance of Oya stone and scratched brick. It is a masterpiece of amazing decoration.
Photo: Masami Tanigawa©

Wright's Architectural Achievements in Japan

1. *Imperial Hotel, Tokyo, 1912*
2. *American Embassy, Tokyo, 1914*
3. *House of Aisaku Hayashi, Tokyo, 1917*
4. *Odawara Hotel, Odawara, 1917*
5. *House of Arinobu Fukuhara, Hakone, 1918*
6. *House of Viscount Tadashiro Inoue, Tokyo, 1918*
7. *Mihara House, Tokyo, 1918*
8. *Movie Theater, Tokyo, 1918*
9. *Yamamura House, Ashiya, 1918*
10. *Annex of Imperial Hotel, Tokyo, 1920*
11. *House of Baron Shinpei Goto, Tokyo, 1921*
12. *Jiyu Gakuen School, Tokyo, 1921*

Some more buildings could be added such as the house of Kodo Shugyo, Hibiya Triangle Building, and the office of the Prime Minister.
Wright's works overseas including proposed plans are only about 32, and more than 12 of them are in Japan. Just 9 works are realized; 6 in Japan and 3 in Canada.
Wright's existing works overseas are merely 4, all of which are in Japan (Imperial Hotel, House of Aisaku Hayashi, Yamamura House and Jiyu Gakuen School Myonichikan). From these facts too, you can understand just how preciuos the Yamamura house is.

years 3 months, from July 1985 to October 1988. The deterioration of the Yamamura House, designated as an Important Cultural Property in 1974, became conspicuous such as decay and breakage of various sections of the building approximately 60 years after its completion.

The second report covers repair carried out over a period of 2 years and 9 months, from June 1995 to March 1998. The House was damaged by the Great Hanshin Earthquake before dawn on 17 January, 1995 necessitating further repairs.

In a way, the Yamamura House was lucky to be repaired twice in just 10 years. However, it is regrettable that we could resist the damage of the earthquake. Survey work was implemented over 9 months before the first repair and, in addition, the defects of the basement around porch were repaired as a supplementary project.

Overcoming the Difficulties of Conservation Consciousness

The second repair construction (disaster recovery) of the Yamamura House was prompt and precise. Seismic strengthening work was implemented by adding a new basement in addition to the expected disaster recovery repair. This demonstrates the sure-footedness of the Cultural Property administration's management of the house.

The first repair construction cost 235 million yen (government subsidy 50%, Hyogo prefecture subsidy 15%, Ashiya city subsidy 15% and the owner's expense 20%). On the contrary, the second disaster recovery construction cost was as huge as 540 million yen (government subsidy 70%, Hyogo prefecture subsidy 10%, Ashiya city subsidy 10%, disaster recovery foundation subsidy 5% and the owner's expense 5%).

林愛作邸
東京、1917年。帝国ホテルの支配人だった林の自邸。

House of Aisaku Hayashi
Tokyo, 1917. Residence for Hayashi, the manager of the Imperial Hotel.

61

発生すれば、大火となり町は灰燼、大きな被害を受けた。地震の発生に至っては、もう成す術もないと、諦観に馴れる生活を繰り返してきた。つまり、災害に弱い環境に住んできたわれわれは、維持や保存は叶わぬこととめつけてきたのである。わが国は、保存のもっとも難しい国だろう。

　古来、営々として造り続けてきた素晴らしい建物を、後世に伝えようという意識は欧米より遅れ、明治期になってようやく定着した。美しい建物、由緒ある建物は保存しなければならないと、重要文化財に指定された建物は膨大な数になった。世界でもきわめて保存条件の難しいわが国で、その悪条件を克服して重要文化財を保護しようという取り組みは、徐々に成果を挙げつつある。

　ライトが日本に遺していった業績の内、4件の建物が遺っている。そして、カナダに建てられた3件の建物が消失した今日、この4件がライトが国外に遺した建物のすべてとなった。彼の母国アメリカに旅行をしなくても、ライトの建物に接することのできる唯一の国というわけである。

　国の重要文化財建造物に指定された旧山邑邸が、指定を契機に「ヨドコウ迎賓館」と呼ばれるようになったことは先にも述べた。ここでいう賓客とは、ここを訪れるお客様一人一人を指している。現在は一般公開されており、住宅建築の巨匠ライトが目指した豊かな住まいを、目で確かめ、直接肌で感じてほしい。

　旧山邑邸は、ライトが渾身の力を注いでデザインした芸術作品であり、今なお多くの人を惹きつける環境に優しい住宅である。

自由学園明日館
東京、1921年
現在は、自由学園明日館。高さを抑え、水平性を強調した草原住宅のスタイルで建てられている。ホールや食堂の木製の窓枠で造られた幾何学模様は質素だが美しい。1997年に国の重要文化財に指定された。
撮影：自由学園明日館©

Jiyu Gakuen School Myonichikan
Tokyo, 1921
Jiyu Gakuen School Myonichikan, at present. Built in the Prairie House design, with a suppressed height and extending horizontal lines. Geometrical patterns of wooden window frames of the auditorium or the dining room are simple but beautiful. This building was designated as a National Important Cultural Property in 1997. Photo: Jiyu Gakuen Myonichikan©

To begin with, ideas about the longevity of architectural structures in Japan and in Western countries completely differ. Buildings made of stone and brick basically do not deteriorate. As long as they don't meet fire or earthquake, they can be thought to last forever. Japan had buildings of wood and paper since before the Edo period. It is understood that they will fall into decay some day even without earthquake or fire. When there is a fire, the damage is huge and a whole city might burn to the ground. As for earthquakes, we had to endure these philosophically as if there was nothing one could do about them. That is, we have determined it would be impossible to maintain or conserve buildings in such a destructive environment. Japan would seem to be a country where it is difficult to preserve architecture.

The awareness of the need to pass on to the next generations the marvelous buildings that have been made over the ages came later than it did in Western countries, and did not finally become entrenched until the Meiji era. There are now countless buildings on the list of Important Properties which enables us to conserve beautiful or historic buildings. Such struggles are gradually showing good results to overcome previous bad conditions and to preserve Important Properties.

Out of the works Wright left in Japan, there still remain four buildings. Now that three buildings by Wright in Canada disappeared, these four are the only buildings Wright left overseas. Japan is the only country where you can touch Wright's architecture without traveling to his home country, USA.

I have already mentioned that the Yamamura House changed its name to "Yodoko Guest House" at the time of its designation as a National Important Cultural Property. Here the term "guest" means each one of the visitors. The building is now open to the public. Please look at and touch this culturally and historically rich residence that Wright, a master of residential architect, aspired to.

The Yamamura House is a work of art that Frank Lloyd Wright designed with all his strength. This environmentally-friendly residence draws a number of people still today.

… World Architecture

Frank Lloyd Wright
Yamamura House
Yodoko Guest House

Text | 谷川正己

建築史家。1930年生まれ。1953年、大阪工業大学建築学科卒。横浜国立大学工学部建築学教室勤務を経て、日本大学工学部の教授を務める。現在は、フランク・ロイド・ライト研究室を主宰。主な著書に『フランク・ロイド・ライト』(鹿島出版会)『フランク・ロイド・ライトとはだれか』(王国社)、訳書に『ライトの遺言』(谷川睦子と共訳)(彰国社) など多数。

Text | Masami Tanigawa

Architectural Historian, born in 1930. Former professor at the College of Engineering, Nihon University.
Now, leading the Masami Tanigawa Studio of Frank Lloyd Wright. Author of "Frank Lloyd Wright". "Road to Taliesin", "Wright and Japan" and others. Translation, "A Testament", "An American Architecture", "The Living City", and others.

Photos | 宮本和義

写真家。1941年上海生まれ。1964年から建築分野、旅分野で活動。著書に『近代建築再見』(エクスナレッジ)、『和風旅館建築の美』『古寺彩彩』(JTB)『近代建築散歩』(小学館) など多数。

Photos | Kazuyoshi Miyamoto

Photographer
Born in Shanghai in 1941
Since 1964, he has been taking architectural and travel photographs.

執筆｜谷川正己©	Text｜© Masami Tanigawa
撮影｜宮本和義©	Photos｜© Kazuyoshi Miyamoto
翻訳｜牧尾晴喜 [スタジオOJMM]©	Translation｜© Haruki Makio (Studio OJMM)
編集｜石原秀一	Chief Editor｜Shuichi Ishihara
大石雄一朗	Staff Editor｜Yuichiro Oishi
デザイン｜堀井知嗣	Design｜Horii Tomotsugu
表紙デザイン｜マルプデザイン	Cover design｜Malpu Design Co.,Ltd.
印刷・製本｜鈴木純司 [モリモト印刷株式会社]	Printer｜Junji Suzuki (MORIMOTO PRINT Co.,Ltd.)
制作協力｜森本起三子 [アトリエM5]	Special Thanks｜Kimiko Morimoto (atelier M5)
株式会社淀川製鋼所	Yodogawa Steel Works, Ltd.
ヨドコウ迎賓館	Yodoko Guest House
自由学園明日館	JIYU GAKUEN MYONICHIKAN
株式会社電通	DENTSU INC.
株式会社藤木工務店	Fujiki Komuten Co.,Ltd.

フランク・ロイド・ライト
旧山邑邸 ヨドコウ迎賓館

2008年4月4日　第1刷発行	First printing April 4, 2008
2011年1月25日　第2刷発行	Revised second printing January 25th, 2011
編集者｜石原秀一	Chief Editor｜Shuichi Ishihara
発行者｜工藤秀之	Publisher｜Hideyuki Kudo
発行所｜バナナブックス©	© Banana Books
株式会社トランスビュー	TRANSVIEW Co.,Ltd.
〒103-0007　東京都中央区日本橋浜町2-10-1-2F	2-10-1-2F, Nihonbashi-Hamacho Chuo-ku, Tokyo, 103-0007 Japan
Tel. 03-3664-7334　Fax. 03-3664-7335	Tel.+81-3-3664-7334　Fax.+81-3-3664-7335
http://www.transview.co.jp/	http://www.transview.co.jp/

2008 BananaBooks, Printed in Japan
All rights reserved
ISBN978-4-902930-17-7